DINGHY COACHING Handbook

This handbook is for all those working, or intending to work, as instructional and coaching staff within the National Sailing Scheme and Racing Coaching Schemes. It replaces previous editions of the G14/G7 logbook. Although the basic principles of teaching sailing have not changed, this edition contains alterations in certain areas reflecting the revision of the RYA National Sailing Scheme in 2002

The RYA is committed to encouraging both men and women to participate in sailing. For clarity only, this book is written using the masculine gender e.g. man overboard.

Text   David Ritchie, James Stevens
Phil Twining and John Driscoll

Cover Photo RS Library

Photos   Ocean Images, RS Library,
Christel clear, David Ritchie,
SW Tourism, Grahame Forshaw,
Sarah Ritchie, Paul Holroyd

Cartoons   Phil Twining and
Jake Kavanagh

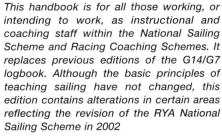

www.rya.org.uk

Published by
The Royal Yachting Association
RYA House Ensign Way Hamble
Southampton SO31 4YA
Tel: 0845 345 0400
Fax: 0845 345 0329
Email: training@rya.org.uk
Web: www.rya.org.uk

FOREWORD

The RYA National Sailing Scheme is taught in a vast number of locations from the open sea to small lakes, from the north of Scotland to the shores of the Mediterranean. The boats vary from Optimists and Picos to keelboats and multihulls including the new generation of high performance asymmetric spinnaker dinghies. In spite of this variation, the process of learning to sail has remained largely unchanged during the thirty years that the RYA has run a national training scheme.

The RYA method known to every dinghy instructor has stood the test of time and with a few modifications remains as effective today as it was at its inception. This book explains the method, including some recent revisions, along with all the other skills and knowledge required by RYA instructors. It assumes you are already a competent sailor who would like to become involved in an RYA recognised centre, teaching dinghy, multihull or keelboat sailing.

This publication includes an explanation of who can teach the scheme and where, and space to include your log of instructional experience.

David Ritchie
RYA National Sailing Coach
March 2003

This book has been improved by contributions from too many people to mention by name. The RYA is particularly grateful to the following for their help in its production:

Nic Wymer for the section on racing instructor training

Dr Roger Herbert for the section on environmental issues

Mike Hart for the section on advanced instructor training

Debbie Brown of RYA Sailability for her section on sailing for the disabled

Simon Davies for the section on teaching single-handed sailing

Andy Carley for the section on learning styles

The National School Sailing Association for permission to reproduce some of the games used in their book *Sailing Across the Curriculum*

Alan Olive and Phil Quill for additional suggestions

Caroline Stevens for reading and correcting the proofs

CONTENTS

EQUAL OPPORTUNITIES
STATEMENT - RYA COACHING

As a National Governing Body of Sport, the RYA fully supports the principles of equal opportunities and is committed to ensure that all participants in its training and coaching schemes are treated fairly and on an equal basis, regardless of gender, age, racial origin, religious persuasion, sexual orientation or disability.

In formulating its schemes and assessment techniques, in operating its procedures and in producing its materials, the RYA seeks to avoid a format, language or approach which:

- Is offensive to members of particular groups

- Cannot be readily understood by some candidates

- Does not have the same meaning for all candidates

- Implies stereotyped or biased attitudes.

The RYA seeks to avoid inequality:

- In the selection, recruitment and training of all those working for or on behalf of the Association

- In the format and content of all syllabi, regulations, assessments and materials produced and/or distributed

- Through the monitoring of its schemes operated at recognised training centres

- By the relaxation of any regulations which serve to inhibit the performance of candidates with special needs in relation to candidates not so disadvantaged, provided that such action does not have a deleterious effect on the standard, quality and integrity of its schemes and assessments.

RYA ORGANISATIONS

CLUBS AFFILIATED TO THE RYA

In order to use the Racing Rules published by ISAF every four years, organising bodies must affiliate to the national governing body. In the UK this is the RYA.

In addition to a range of other benefits, racing certificates in the Youth Sailing Scheme can be issued in such clubs when an appropriately qualified person delivers coaching.

RYA CHAMPION CLUBS

The RYA has created an award that looks to encourage and stimulate Junior racing in RYA recognised classes. The benefits of joining the scheme provide a hallmark of quality racing. The process is run by the RYA High Performance Managers. All details are listed on the RYA website.

A Champion Club is required to:

- Provide a structured Junior Race Training Programme in one of the RYA Recognised Junior Classes, which are Optimist, Topper, Mirror and Cadet.
- Guide their promising youngsters into the recognised youth classes following their period in a junior class.
- Have sufficient numbers of a recognised junior class of boat (members or club owned), equipment and qualified personnel to achieve the aims of partnership.

RYA TRAINING CENTRES

Only recognised centres can issue RYA certificates,(except for Youth Sailing Scheme Racing Badges). These centres fall into three main categories:

- Sailing centres open to the public
- Sailing clubs providing tuition for their members and prospective members
- Organisations such as local education authorities, Scouts and HM Services, who are restricted to teaching their own groups or members.

RYA recognition is vested in the Principal and the site and implies that certificated courses are run and that the remainder are closely associated with the aims of the National Sailing Scheme. The Principal is responsible for issuing RYA certificates and ensuring that the requirements of RYA recognition are maintained at all times.

An initial application fee is payable by all new recognised centres. Thereafter, an annual subscription is payable to the RYA, except in the case of centres who are already subscribing as affiliated clubs or associations.

Full details of the recognition procedure and requirements are available from the RYA along with a pack containing more in depth information for new and prospective Principals.

In summary, each dinghy or keelboat centre will be inspected annually to ascertain that:

- The Principal or Chief Instructor holds a valid RYA Senior or Keelboat Instructor certificate as appropriate

- The instructors hold the appropriate valid RYA instructor certificates

- The student to instructor ratios do not exceed those laid down in the syllabus for each level of course:

- The training centre's teaching syllabus meets the requirements of RYA certificate courses

Type of craft	Student to instructor ratio:
Crewed dinghies/multihulls with instructor on board	3:1
Single handed dinghies	6:1 (applies only whilst the boats are used as single-handers)
Keelboats	*Keelboats with accommodation* 5:1 (Instructor on board) *Dayboats/keelboats without accommodation* Maximum 4 students per boat.
Dinghy general	1 instructor must be responsible for no more than 9 students (eg 3 boats with 3 students in each boat or 4 boats with 2 students in each)

- The onshore teaching facilities are adequate for the proposed operation

- Boats provided for tuition are suitable, seaworthy and in good repair

- Safety boats satisfy all the requirements for the operating area and are properly equipped to carry out the combined duties of teaching platform and rescue boat

- All students and instructors will be in possession of personal buoyancy appropriate to the sailing area and type of boat in which they are receiving instruction, and will be required to wear this equipment on occasions when prevailing conditions make its use necessary

- The Principal understands the requirements of the RYA as to the proper running of a recognised training centre

- The Principal understands his responsibilities for training his staff in teaching techniques, powerboat handling and house rules relating to health and safety issues

- All activities will be covered by adequate public liability insurance (at least £2,000,000)

- RYA logbooks will be available to all students and RYA certificates will be issued to all those who successfully complete the course.

Recognition of Overseas Centres

Sailing centres permanently based outside the United Kingdom must primarily teach in English. The centres shall pay the overseas recognition fee and the costs of annual inspection visits, including transport, accommodation and subsistence. All other requirements for UK centres apply.

Withdrawal of Recognition

The RYA Training Committee can withdraw recognition for contravention of the rules or spirit of recognition.

A school wishing to appeal against withdrawal of recognition may bring their case to an RYA panel, which will be convened for the purpose.

For more information on RYA recognition see the Guidance Notes for Inspections of RYA Training Centres.

HOW TO APPLY FOR RYA RECOGNITION

Please refer to the Guidance Notes for full details of the requirements for recognition. If you wish to make an application, follow the procedure shown below:

Principal or Chief instructor holds appropriate RYA qualification

Complete the application for recognition and send it to the RYA with the fee. Also send your credit account application form if you wish to open an account for buying publications.

The RYA will send you a copy of your application for recognition to your regional coach or liaison officer who will nominate an inspector and contact you to arrange a date for inspection.

Complete the shaded sections of the Centre Inspection Report form and keep it ready for the inspector to complete the rest.

Your inspector will need to see some training in action. The training could be, for example, an introductory session for some volunteers or in house training for staff. The inspector will be looking for good standards of tuition, safety and supervision.

On satisfactory completion of an inspection, the report will be sent to RYA HQ with a recommendation to grant recognition, which will be confirmed to the Principal.

If you need further advice on applying for recognition, contact either the Training Division at RYA HQ or your Regional Coach/Liaison Officer. When you have been allocated an Inspector, they will also be able to offer advice prior to their visit.

Advertising

Recognised centres may use the RYA logo, details of which are available from the RYA. Centres must ensure that they do not use the name of the RYA to advertise any activities not covered by the terms of recognition.

Swimmers

It is recommended that all those participating in the sport of sailing should be able to swim. No minimum level swimming ability is stipulated, but students should be able to demonstrate water confidence. It is essential that the instructor in charge of a course know if any course members are non-swimmers. Non-swimmers may be required to wear life jackets instead of buoyancy aids.

Duty of Care

Instructors must always remember that they are usually teaching relatively inexperienced sailors, who may not be able to make a sound assessment of the risks inherent in the sport. Instructors should not hesitate to make prudent decisions in unfavourable conditions.

In order that they are informed as any additional risk to students, RYA training centres are strongly advised to include a health declaration in their booking forms. The Principal must pass on such information to the individual instructor responsible for the student.

The declaration should say that the student is, to the best of their knowledge, not suffering from epilepsy, disability, giddy spells, asthma, angina, or other heart condition, and is fit to participate in the course. It should be signed and dated by the student and include details of any medical conditions or injuries and medication being taken. If there is doubt as to someone's fitness to take part, medical advice may be sought.

Instructors must themselves declare to the RYA any medical condition, such as one of these listed above, which is likely to affect their ability to carry out a duty of care.

I WANT TO BE AN INSTRUCTOR OR COACH

WHO TEACHES WHAT...

in the RYA National Sailing and Youth Sailing Scheme**

| | NATIONAL SAILING SCHEME | | | YOUTH SAILING SCHEME |
	Dinghies	Keelboats	Multihulls	
Dinghy Instructor	Levels 1 & 2, Day Sailing, Seamanship Skills Sailing with Spinnakers*			Stage 1, 2, 3 Advanced Red and White in dinghies
Keelboat Instructor		Levels 1 & 2, Day Sailing, Seamanship Skills Sailing with Spinnakers*		Stage 1, 2, 3 Advanced Red and White in Keelboats
Multihull Instructor			Levels 1 & 2, Day Sailing, Seamanship Skills Sailing with Spinnakers*	Stage 1, 2, 3 Advanced Red and White in Multihulls
Advanced Instructor	As instructor plus Sailing with Spinnakers, Performance Sailing	Sailing with Spinnakers, Performance Sailing. Should be Keelboat instructor	Sailing with Spinnakers, Performance Sailing. Should be Multihull instructor	As Instructor plus Advanced Blue
Racing Instructor	As instructor plus Start Racing			As Instructor plus Racing Red
Club Racing Coach	Start Racing			Racing Red and White
Class Racing Coach	Start Racing			As Club Racing Coach plus Racing Blue
Yachtmaster Instructor		As instructor		

10

and in Instructor and Coach Training

	Course	Ratio	Moderator
Senior Instructor	Assistant Instructor		
Coach/Assessor	Dinghy Instructor	1:6	Yes
	Keelboat Instructor***	1:6	Yes
	Multihull Instructor***	1:6	Yes
	Dinghy endorsement	1:6	
	Multihull endorsement***	1:6	
	Keelboat endorsement***	1:6	
	Coastal endorsement	1:6	
	Advanced endorsement	1:6	
	Racing endorsement	1:6	
	Senior Instructor	Minimum 6 candidates	Throughout course
Club Racing Coach Tutor	Club Racing Coach	Maximum 8 candidates	
Coaching Development Manager	Class Racing Coach		National Racing Coach
Coaching Development Manager	Club Racing Coach Tutor		

* Instructor who is experienced with spinnakers and approved by the Principal or Chief Instructor.

** All RYA tuition must be supervised by a Senior Instructor

*** Coach/Assessor approved by National Sailing Coach

I WANT TO BE ....

AN ASSISTANT INSTRUCTOR

Sailing Standard	Pass one National Sailing Scheme Advanced Module
Recommendation	By Principal of Training Centre
Attend	Two day course at the centre run by Senior Instructor

AN RYA INSTRUCTOR

Minimum age	16 years
Powerboat	National Powerboat Certificate Level 2
First Aid	Relevant First Aid Certificate
Sailing ability	To correct standard
	Pre-entry Sailing Assessment
Do Course	Attend five-day instructor training course run by RYA Coach/Assessor, with continuous assessment, and moderation by another Coach/Assessor

A CLUB RACING COACH

Minimum age	16 (18 if working unsupervised)
First Aid	Relevant First Aid Certificate
Powerboat	National Powerboat Certificate Level 2
Do Course	Attend two-day training course run by Club Racing Coach Tutor
Certification fee	Free to RYA members
	Attend *Top Mark* within 1 year of training course

Health Declaration

RYA Instructors and Coaches must declare any medical condition which might affect their duty of care as an instructor. This includes any relevant change in their medical situation after qualifying.

The RYA reserves the right to withhold or suspend qualification from anyone who is considered unlikely to fulfil this requirement.

I ALSO WANT TO GET AN NVQ

The process of obtaining an NVQ for dinghy instruction can be started at any time during or after the process above. Further details can be found on page 116

REQUIREMENTS FOR RYA INSTRUCTOR AND COACHING AWARDS

ASSISTANT INSTRUCTOR AWARD

This award provides recognition of the local training given to experienced sailors intending to qualify as RYA Dinghy or Keelboat Instructors.

Role

The Assistant Instructor is a competent small boat sailor, who has been trained to assist Instructors with teaching sailing up to the standard of the National Sailing Certificate Level 2 and the Start Sailing Stages 1, 2 and 3 of the Youth Sailing Scheme. They must work under the supervision of an RYA Senior Instructor (for dinghy sailing centres) or the Chief Instructor of a keelboat training centre.

Eligibility

Candidates must hold one of the National Sailing Scheme advanced modules or Youth Sailing Scheme Advanced White Badge.

Training

Training and assessment are conducted by the Principal or Chief Instructor of an RYA training centre who holds a valid RYA Senior Instructor certificate (for dinghy sailing centres). The training may be based on a 20-hour course covering the RYA teaching methods for beginners outlined on page 50

Assessment

Candidates will be assessed on their practical teaching ability with beginners. Successful candidates will have their Log signed and will be awarded an RYA Assistant Instructor certificate by their Principal.

Certificate Validity

The Assistant Instructor Certificate awarded to successful candidates is valid only at that centre for five years.

Important Note

As the training and assessment is limited to the role of assisting qualified instructors and does not include first aid or powerboat handling, Assistant Instructors must never be allowed to work without direct supervision.

It is normal practice for every Principal to ensure that all his staff are conversant with the teaching techniques and local 'house rules' of that centre. Thus if an Assistant Instructor moves from one training centre to another, it is likely that his new Principal will issue a new Assistant Instructor Award after retraining.

DINGHY/KEELBOAT/MULTIHULL INSTRUCTOR

It is possible to complete the National Sailing Scheme in dinghies, keelboats or multihulls. Instructors teaching the scheme must be qualified for the type of boat in which they will be teaching, i.e. only RYA Dinghy Instructors can teach in dinghies, and only RYA Keelboat Instructors can teach in keelboats. The instructor certificate is endorsed accordingly and will also show whether the instructor is qualified to teach on inland or coastal waters (depending on where they completed the pre-entry sailing assessment and course).

Role

The Instructor is a competent and experienced small boat sailor, capable of sailing a training boat confidently in strong winds and handling small powerboats. The Instructor has been assessed as competent to teach dinghy or keelboat sailing to adults and children, both beginners and improvers, including the RYA National Sailing Scheme Level 1 and Level 2, Seamanship Skills, and Youth Sailing Scheme Stage 1 to 3 and Advanced Red/White badges.

Although responsible for teaching individuals and small groups, the Instructor has not been assessed as competent in running a sailing school, and should always work under the supervision of an RYA Senior Instructor (for dinghy/multihull courses) or the Chief Instructor of a keelboat-training centre.

Eligibility

Candidates must fulfil the following criteria before taking part in the instructor training course:

Minimum age 16 (no candidates will be accepted for training under this age)

Valid first aid certificate: either the RYA First Aid Course, or one recognised by the Health and Safety Executive, covering the treatment of hypothermia and a minimum of six hours course length

RYA Powerboat Level 2 certificate

Pre-entry sailing assessment completed within one year prior to the instructor training course in the appropriate type of boat (details given on page 47).

Training

Training in teaching techniques afloat and ashore is provided during the instructor training course, which is staffed by RYA Coach/Assessors. The course will be based on a five-day week of 50 hours, but may take the form of a number of weekends, single days or sessions at the discretion of the organiser. Courses run in this way on a protracted basis may take slightly longer than the 50 hours to allow for revision time. Candidates should apply to RYA HQ or their Regional Coach for a list of instructor courses.

The course will include:

a) The structure of the National Scheme

b) Training in RYA teaching methods to the Seamanship Skills Module including teaching those with special needs

c) Instructing techniques for adults and children

d) Preparation and presentation of a lesson

e) Preparation and use of visual aids

f) Teaching racing

g) The assessment of students' abilities

h) The revision of all subjects covered in Levels 1 & 2 and Seamanship Skills

i) A one-hour written paper (or oral test) covering teaching methods and background knowledge

j) The use of powered craft in a teaching environment

Throughout the course, evidence of competence in these areas will be noted by the training Coach/Assessor and credited towards the candidate's final moderation/assessment.

Moderation/Assessment

The moderation will usually take place on the final day of the training course and will be carried out by a Coach/Assessor who has not been involved in or associated with the training of the candidates. Candidates will be required to demonstrate competence in the following areas:

Course preparation

Course delivery

Course management

Customer liaison

The moderation will take place in a conventional teaching environment, preferably using real beginners as students.

Certificate Validity

Instructor certificates are valid for five years from the date of issue, provided that a valid first aid certificate is maintained. Every five years a Revalidation Form must be obtained from RYA Headquarters which should be completed and returned, with the Instructor Certificate, for revalidation along with a log of instruction experience in RYA Training Centres since qualifying, details of current first aid certificate and the appropriate fee or RYA membership number. If little or no experience is shown, it may be necessary for the instructor to attend a re-assessment in order to ensure that the instructor is up to date with current practice. In normal circumstances revalidation of the Instructor award includes all instructor endorsements.

Note

It is possible for instructors to complete their training course in multihulls and have their certificates endorsed to show that they are Multihull Instructors. However, the more common route to obtaining this qualification is to first qualify as a Dinghy Instructor and then complete a two-day Multihull endorsement course. Please see the following section on instructor endorsements.

INSTRUCTOR ENDORSEMENTS

An RYA Instructor can teach students the modules Level 1, Level 2, and Seamanship Skills of the National Sailing Scheme, and Youth Sailing Scheme up to Advanced White. He can also teach Sailing with Spinnakers with the approval of the Principal and Day Sailing under the supervision of a coastal SI. The following endorsements are designed to extend the scope of an instructor's ability and will increase his value to the Principal of a training centre.

COASTAL ENDORSEMENT

Role

Instructors who completed their initial training course and assessment inland, but who subsequently want to instruct at a coastal establishment should obtain this endorsement. Training Centres in the Mediterranean are classified as coastal.

A coastal endorsement to the instructor award applies to all other instructor endorsements, including the Advanced Instructor. However, Senior Instructors wishing to operate at a coastal venue must hold a coastal SI award.

Training

Candidates should apply to their Regional Coach for details of courses. Training will be given by an RYA Coach/Assessor. Candidates will be required to attend a two-day training course or a one day assessment, during which they should demonstrate the pre-entry sailing test skills and teaching techniques in tidal waters.

Assessment

Candidates will be assessed on a continuous basis afloat by the training Coach/Assessor. Upon successful completion of the course, that Coach/Assessor will sign their logbooks.

ADVANCED ENDORSEMENT

Role

The Advanced Instructor is an experienced instructor with a wide background of sailing experience who has been trained to teach the RYA National Sailing Scheme Performance Sailing and Sailing with Spinnakers Courses, and Youth Sailing Scheme Advanced Blue.

Eligibility

Candidates will hold the RYA Instructor certificate and will usually have recorded at least one season's experience of teaching sailing since obtaining that certificate. Candidates will be skilled to at least the level of the requirements of the Performance Sailing and Sailing with Spinnakers Courses and should have previous powerboat handling experience in a teaching environment.

Training

Candidates should apply to their Regional Coach for details of courses. Candidates will be required to attend a two-day course covering the teaching of boat handling, the use of spinnakers and 5 essentials coaching to the required standard, as well as powerboat driving.

Assessment

Candidates will be assessed on a continuous basis afloat, and may be given a theory test. Upon successful completion of the course, the Coach/Assessor will sign their logbooks.

KEELBOAT/MULTIHULL ENDORSEMENT

Role

Instructors who completed their initial training course and assessment in dinghies, but who subsequently want to instruct in small keelboats or multihulls respectively should obtain these endorsements.

Training

Candidates should apply to their Regional Coach for details of courses. Training will be given by an RYA Coach/Assessor with relevant experience, and who has been authorised by the RYA to run such Instructor training. Candidates will be required to attend a two-day course during which they should demonstrate the pre-entry test skills and teaching techniques.

Assessment

Candidates will be assessed on a continuous basis afloat. Upon successful completion of the course, the course organiser will sign their logbooks.

RACING ENDORSEMENT

Role

This endorsement should be obtained by instructors with experience of club racing who wish to teach racing skills at Red Badge level in the RYA Youth Sailing Scheme and to run the Start Racing module of The National Sailing Scheme.

Eligibility

Dinghy instructor trainees who have experience of club racing (minimum completed 8 races and assistant race officer role once) may qualify during their Instructor Training course or, as qualified dinghy instructors, may undertake further training at a later time by a Coach Assessor.

Training

Candidates should apply to their Regional Coach for details of courses, which will include the organisation of club racing, preparation and management of the Start Racing and Red Badge courses and instructional technique afloat including the use of race training exercises.

CLUB RACING COACH

Role

The Club Racing Coach is an experienced racing sailor who has been trained to teach and coach racing skills at Red and White Badge level in the RYA Youth Sailing Scheme, to run the Start Racing module of The National Sailing Scheme at clubs/training centres, and to assist RYA Class Racing Coaches. A Club Racing Coach does not have to be an RYA Instructor.

Eligibility

Five years racing experience

Active club racer who has who has recently attended a National Championship or equivalent.

RYA Powerboat Level 2 certificate.

Valid first aid certificate: either the RYA First Aid Course, or one recognised by the Health and Safety Executive, including the treatment of hypothermia. Minimum course length of six hours.

Minimum age 16. Club Racing Coaches aged under 18 should be appropriately supervised by an adult.

Training

Candidates should approach their High Performance Manager or class representative for details of courses. A Club Racing Coach Tutor provides training.

An application form is available via the RYA website www.rya.org.uk

Candidates will be required to attend a two-day course covering methods for coaching, running exercises, de-briefing, and designing race training programmes. All candidates are required to attend a Top Mark Conference within a year of attending their course.

Resources available from the RYA include the Club Racing Coach workbook and CD.

Revalidation:

Every 3 years at the Top Mark Zone Conference run by the HPM.

CLASS RACING COACH

Role

The Racing Coach is a highly experienced, accomplished racing sailor, capable of running class association racing clinics and Youth Racing Blue Badge courses within the RYA Youth Sailing Scheme.

Eligibility

Club Racing Coach with at least one year's experience who has competed with distinction at regional, national or international regattas. Candidates should have assisted a Class Racing Coach or with RYA Squad training.

First aid requirement as for Club Racing Coach

National Powerboat Certificate Level 2

Candidates should apply to the Coaching Development Manager, and their application should be endorsed by a Class Association, National Coach or High Performance Manager.

Award

To achieve the award, candidates should complete the following accreditation process:

Attendance at the Class Racing Coaches Course

To have coached for at least 6 months after the course

Assessment weekend working with a National Coach

Attendance at the *Top Mark* annual conference

Resources

Class Racing Coach Workbook and CD

Revalidation

The award must be completed within two years of attending the training course, or the course should be repeated. All coaches should attend an annual *Top Mark* Conference every three years from the award of their qualifications.

SENIOR INSTRUCTOR

Role

The Senior Instructor is an experienced instructor who has been assessed as competent to organise and manage sailing courses within the RYA National Sailing Scheme.

The Senior Instructor is qualified to organise and control group sailing tuition and to supervise and assist instructors. Such a person must be a confident, competent manager, capable of organising groups of all ages and directing the work of his instructors.

An RYA recognised dinghy/keelboat/multihull training centre must have a current Senior Instructor as its Principal or Chief Sailing Instructor, though a Yachtmaster Instructor may fulfil this role in a keelboat centre.

Eligibility

Candidates must first be an RYA Dinghy Instructor and must fulfil the following criteria before taking part in the Senior Instructor training course:

Minimum age 18

Two years intermittent or one year full time dinghy instructing since qualifying

RYA Safety Boat certificate.

Valid first aid certificate: either the RYA First Aid Course, or one recognised by the Health and Safety Executive, covering the treatment of hypothermia and a minimum of six hours course length.

Signed recommendation from the Principal of an RYA training centre (see page 126).

During the course candidates will be asked to demonstrate that they have sailing ability to at least the standard of an RYA Dinghy Instructor.

Training

Candidates should apply to their Regional Coach for details of courses, which are run on a regional basis with a minimum of six students. Courses are organised through the Regional Coach and staffed by two or more RYA Coach/Assessors. The course may take the form of two weekends (four whole days) and include some material covered prior to the course.

Assessment

The assessment will be continuous and will be made by at least two Coach/Assessors. Candidates will be required to demonstrate competence in the following areas:

Personal sailing ability

Centre administration

Course preparation, delivery and management

Customer liaison

Certificate Validity

Senior Instructor certificates are valid for five years from the date of issue, provided that a valid first aid certificate is maintained. Every five years a Revalidation Form must be obtained from RYA Headquarters which should be completed and returned, with the Instructor Certificate, for revalidation along with a log of instruction experience in RYA Training Centres since qualifying, details of current first aid certificate and the appropriate fee or RYA membership number. If little or no experience is shown, it may be necessary to attend a re-assessment in order to ensure that the instructor is up to date with current practice. In normal circumstances revalidation of the award includes all instructor endorsements.

COACH /ASSESSOR

A Coach/Assessor is an experienced Senior and Advanced Instructor who has been trained and assessed as competent to themselves train and assess Instructors and Senior Instructors, and appointed to deliver such training by the National Coach. Coach/Assessors are appointed on an annual basis, and attend an update every five years.

Eligibility

A Senior Instructor with proven ability. These qualities are expected to include a thoroughly competent level of personal sailing ability, good teaching, motivating and leadership skills, good fleet management and coaching, and a positive enthusiastic approach based on good communication skills.

A mature approach is necessary. Training candidate instructors can be a challenging business, demanding delicate judgement.

Regional Coaches nominate potential Coach/Assessors to the National Coach.

Coach/Assessors based overseas are occasionally trained where a requirement can be demonstrated. In this case the first approach should be to the RYA HQ.

Coach/Assessor Training

This consists of three parts:

Preparation/selection weekend

Five-day training course

Apprenticeship

Preparation/selection weekend

Candidates should be able to:

Demonstrate and teach any part of the National Sailing Scheme including all the modules.

Sail competently in a variety of dinghies including single-handers and high performance craft

Plan and manage a course involving sessions ashore and afloat

Handle a safety boat and coach boat

Give a formal presentation including the use of visual aids, and chair a discussion

Show enthusiasm, motivation and leadership

Training course

The training course will include:

The skills of teaching and assessing RYA Dinghy Instructors.

The RYA National Sailing Scheme and standards required for instructional awards including the administration of the scheme

Advanced seamanship techniques

High performance dinghy sailing

Techniques of Senior Instructor training

Teaching students with special needs

Apprenticeship

Candidates who complete the course successfully will normally be invited to work with an experienced Coach/Assessor until their Regional Coach makes a recommendation that they should be appointed.

Coach/Assessors wishing to train Keelboat or Multihull Instructors should normally attend a separate course organised by the RYA.

Coaches wishing to become Inspectors of training centres should attend a one-day training course organised by the RYA.

Coach/Assessor Updating

After 5 years Coach/Assessors must attend a short practical updating course organised by the RYA. The update will include:

• Techniques for teaching and assessing instructors

• Information on changes to the scheme

• An opportunity to feed back to the RYA

• A personal sailing test

TECHNIQUES FOR INSTRUCTING AND COACHING

INSTRUCTING AND COACHING SKILLS

Sailing instruction is essentially a practical process of brief – task – debrief. The students are there to handle the equipment and actually do the tasks.

The learning really starts afloat and in particular when the student takes the helm. The instructor's job is to make this experience enjoyable, informative and safe.

On a course you should start sailing as soon as possible. A safety brief, correct clothes and a demonstration are essential but don't spend time talking about the theory of sailing at this stage. Students are usually slightly anxious about their first sail and stories about dangers and disasters will do little to allay their fears. Once people see the boat and equipment being used, or better still, are using it themselves they will pick up the concept fairly quickly. Also, the sooner you can give a student a straightforward achievable task followed by a genuine 'well done', the sooner they will relax and realise the course is achievable.

TOP TIP

Always summarise for clarity.

Clear summaries help both instructor and student

Briefing

You must be able to explain clearly what is required. This is virtually impossible across the water from a moving powerboat or to a frightened student in a heeling dinghy. Brief ashore or, if afloat, calm down the situation by lying to or heaving to.

A demonstration is an excellent way of showing the task required. The National Sailing Scheme incorporates a progression of demonstrations, some of them ashore (the land drills), which allow students to observe and then handle the controls without any distractions. When giving a demonstration make sure everyone can see and then draw their attention to the part of the boat that is important at the time. This might be the tiller, the luff of the jib, or possibly the sideways effect of the tide.

WELL, LITTLE BEN AINSLIE WAS **BEGGING** FOR MY ADVICE.

Make your briefings exactly that - brief. The anecdotes can come later, and remember the purpose of the demonstration is to teach a new skill not to display your prowess. Your brief has failed if the students are unclear about what they are supposed to be doing. Good instructors can deliver and summarise the brief as a succession of related 'bullet points' which are clear and easy to remember. A few questions at the end will help to reinforce the points made.

At more advanced levels it can be a good idea to involve the sailors in the brief using brainstorming and questions. Check their knowledge before going afloat. It can also be useful to encourage students to set their own goals for each session.

The Task

The task must be chosen to suit the ability of the student. Part of the skill of instructing is to assess the student's ability and provide tuition at a challenging but not impossible level. It is very frustrating for someone with a natural flair or with some experience to be taught at the pace of the slowest beginner.

Once the task has been set, allow the student to feel responsible for it. Do not continually interrupt - if you have briefed well it should be unnecessary. If events start to go wrong a quiet word will allow the student to correct the mistake while still being in control. Never elbow students out of the way to demonstrate your skill; the idea is that they demonstrate theirs.

Occasionally, if you can, allow a mistake to be made to illustrate a point, but only do this if you feel it is a good learning opportunity. It is a technique more appropriate to the higher level courses and you should take great care not to use the situation to put down or demoralise the student.

Debriefing

Debriefing is one of the most important skills of the sailing instructor. Done well it is informative, positive, good-natured and helpful. Done badly it can be destructive and demoralising. At the end of a debrief the students should be clear about what happened, their strengths and weaknesses, and be fired with enthusiasm to try again. They should never lose their self esteem or motivation.

Debrief as soon as possible after the task. If you are in the boat with the students, heave to. If you are teaching single handlers, stop regularly.

You must observe each task very carefully both to give feedback to individuals as well as the group. A notebook is helpful if you are in a safety boat or ashore but can be a bit 'official' and threatening in a dinghy. Don't overload the students with information but keep your feedback focused on what the session was about.

The most useful information a sailor receives is from himself, so a good way of debriefing is to ask the students what happened or if they would act differently next time. Your comments should reinforce what was done well but you must also be clear about what needs improvement. The instructor's personality comes in here. It is important to be able to deliver advice on how to correct mistakes without any 'edge' or bad feeling. Students want to know what they did wrong but do not want to be 'ticked off' or feel their instructor is using the occasion to deliver a personal slight.

STUDENTS DON'T LIKE BEING 'TICKED OFF'....

The standard form of debrief starts with a recognition of what went well followed by the errors made and finishes with encouragement on how to improve. A few questions will give the student an opportunity to give their point of view and ensure that the instructor knows that the point has been received. The best coaches and instructors enable the sailor to become their own coach. Many instructors used to taking charge and issuing commands neglect the students' own comments. They are therefore unaware as to whether they are learning anything.

There are many models for debriefing but the traffic light is an effective one.

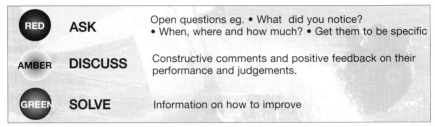

RED	**ASK**	Open questions eg. • What did you notice? • When, where and how much? • Get them to be specific
AMBER	**DISCUSS**	Constructive comments and positive feedback on their performance and judgements.
GREEN	**SOLVE**	Information on how to improve

Providing Feedback

Open questions initiate dialogue. Try to use them to encourage discussion. The following words are the prefixes for open questions, which should be used whenever possible in eliciting feedback from your students:

• Why?   • Who?   • Where?   • What?   • How?

The following words generally prefix closed questions:

• Did?   • Should?   • Will?   • Is?

These are likely to return answers of limited value, such as *Yes* or *No*.

Try to provide each student with regular, encouraging feedback, which helps them to improve. Look for something positive to say first (however awful the attempt at a skill has been) and then tell them how to improve. Avoid sarcasm or negativity at all times.

Non-verbal messages

• Try to motivate your students. Check that you are giving each student equal attention and encourage their concentration.

• Much of our best communication is not spoken, including head-nods, smiles, frowns, physical contact, eye movements, laughter, body posture, language and many other actions.

• The eyes are crucial – take your sunglasses off if possible. Glazed or down-turned eyes indicate boredom or disinterest, as does fidgeting, which may also signal disagreement. Fully raised eyebrows signal disbelief and half raised indicate puzzlement.

• You may be able to gauge the mood and attitude of your group by observation, so try to be aware of the signals being transmitted by your students.

Occasionally allow a mistake to be made....

WE'RE GYBING – NOTHING TO WORRY...

Methods, motivators and barriers to learning

Adults and young people often learn in different ways and for different reasons:

As an Instructor, try to be aware of your students' motivation for taking part and organise your delivery accordingly. In addition, be aware that people often bring their own barriers to learning: other responsibilities, feeling cold, lack of self confidence or a personality clash with the instructor may feature. "I'm here because I have to be, not because I want to be" is a common issue for young people. The imaginative instructor will find ways to address these issues.

Adults	Young People
Self directed	More random and instructor led
Goals and structure are important	Fun and experiential approach
Need to know why they are learning something	More need for the what, where and when rather than why
Often apply previous experience	May be experiencing the skill for the first time. Uninhibited - like to be with their friends

How do we teach a new skill?

Sailing involves a number of different skills. These include thinking skills (cognitive), the ability to interpret information, and movement skills (kinaesthetic). You will usually require more than one way to be fully successful in communicating a skill. These may include:

TOP TIP

I hear, I forget
I see, I understand
I do, I remember

• Demonstrations, verbal instructions and experience (try it)

• Video, diagrams photo sequences

• Images or visualisation

....so long as it's not too serious.

... ABOUT ?

Demonstrations are particularly important and useful in sailing, so demonstrate whenever possible. People will need time to identify what is being taught, link the parts into a smooth skill and become automatic.

This leads us to the 'whole – part – whole' demonstration method, where the skill is executed at normal speed, then broken into detailed parts, then redone at normal speed. In this way both a mental picture and a detailed understanding can be conveyed.

How to remember skills and instructions

A mnemonic is a vivid image, story or rhyme which helps you to remember a complicated skill or process (such as tacking). Many people find these helpful, particularly if they are easy to remember for some reason:

- Use positive, pleasant images and exaggerate the size of important parts of the image "Crouch down like a mouse"

- Use humour and rhyming. Funny things are easier to remember.

- Vivid images and symbols can be helpful. (West Cardinal Buoy has a Waist)

Land Drills

- Sailing can be seen as a series of drills.

- Land drills introduce clarity and simplicity. They enable students to achieve more in less time afloat. They are not an end in themselves, nor are they always appropriate

- Introduce the session by explaining why the land drill may be useful

- Make it as real as possible. Boats are much better than ropes and chairs

- If using a boat, make sure it is safe on its trolley with people aboard, or put it on grass.

- Position the students where they can see clearly but are safe. Be aware of any distractions

- What you do is more important than what you say. Use few words and demonstrate smoothly at normal speed, before breaking the manoeuvre down

- Most people talk too much as they demonstrate

- Involve your students where possible e.g. in moving the boom or balancing the boat

- When teaching children, consider increasing entertainment by turning the drill into play by the use of songs or other ideas

- Land drills are useful for a number of skills e.g. spinnaker work, anchoring, reefing etc., where a complicated series of actions have to be co-ordinated

REMEMBER —
SHARP LOOKOUT,
ALL THE TIME !

How our students learn

People learn in many different ways. They may have very different preferences to you for how, when, and where they learn. It is your responsibility to enable your students to learn, rather than just to teach the material.

Just as most people have a preference for using their left or right hands, they tend to have a preferred learning style.

Adults and children usually learn in different ways. If sailors are aware of their preferred style, they can vary or adapt their approach to learning. As an Instructor or Coach it is a good idea to modify and vary your style and approach to suit your students.

The three major ways in which people learn new things are:

• Visual (seeing)

• Auditory (hearing)

• Kinaesthetic (active doing)

Visual Learners

Visual learners relate well to written information: notes, diagrams and pictures. Typically they will be unhappy with a presentation where they are unable to take detailed notes - to an extent information does not exist for a visual learner unless it has been seen written down. This is why some visual learners will take notes even when they have printed course notes such as this book. Visual learners will tend to be most effective in written communication, symbol manipulation etc.

Auditory Learners

Auditory learners relate most effectively to the spoken word. They will tend to listen to a lecture, and then take notes afterwards, or rely on printed notes. Often information written down will have little meaning until it has been heard - it may help auditory learners to read written information out loud. (Auditory learners may be sophisticated speakers, and may specialise effectively in subjects like law or politics.)

Kinaesthetic Learners (Movement)

Kinaesthetic learners learn effectively through touch, movement and space: they learn skills by imitation and practice. Kinaesthetic learners can appear slow, in that usually information is not presented in a style that suits their learning methods.

Each person may well use more than one style and preferences may change as skill develops. Use all styles and judge the reaction to see which is most effective.

Keeping students informed

RYA certificates provide a great incentive to book on courses. However they can become a discouragement to the weak student as the prospect of a certificate fades. Your Chief Instructor will advise on the importance of keeping everyone informed as to their progress through the course, and what they can realistically achieve. So this could involve breaking the news that a Performance Sailing certificate is not possible by the end of the course. Explain what can be achieved and agree between you to get the best possible value out of the course.

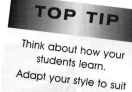

TOP TIP

Think about how your students learn. Adapt your style to suit

From then on set goals, point out strengths and weaknesses and offer encouragement. Point out how much has been achieved as the course progresses so that by the final debrief you can both be satisfied that the course was worthwhile.

If you fail to keep students informed, tension will build up with students discussing amongst themselves whether they are passing or failing. During the final debrief your teaching may be blamed for lack of results. This lack of communication between instructor and student is one of the most common reasons for complaints about RYA courses. Remember that many of the people you teach are highly successful and respected in their own field. The only skill you may have that they haven't is the ability to sail and teach sailing. Try to ensure they retain their dignity and a positive attitude towards you and the sport. This is one of the most skillful aspects of instructing.

Your first course

Your best plan is to arrive early and get to know the area and boats. Your Chief Instructor will ensure you know the 'house rules' and where the equipment is stowed. Make a list of the points you wish to make during the teaching session.

When the students arrive, welcome them and ask them about themselves and their background and experience. Learn their names immediately. Explain what you are going to do and invite them to ask about anything they do not understand. If you come across as sincere, the students will be willing you to succeed, even if your teaching technique is unpolished. Be honest about your own experience.

Avoid giving them an over-inflated view of yourself or you will lose their confidence.

If you make an error admit it, think clearly and put it right. No-one gives perfect demonstrations every time but you should be able to stay in control and correct mis-judgements.

Being slightly nervous before your first course is a good quality - it shows you care and want to make it a success. At the end, thinking of the things you should have done during the course is also a good quality - it means you are evaluating and improving what you do.

The Principal of the centre is there to give you help and advice. Use it.

Ten Instructor Qualities

COMPETENT SAILOR
Not necessarily brilliant, but capable, competent and reassuring

GOOD COMMUNICATOR
Articulate and clear, good listener, doesn't continually talk about themselves and comes across as interested and approachable

GOOD TEACHER
Can explain clearly using visual aids where necessary, can structure a lesson

COACH
Can assess progress and provide individual goals and tuition

HONEST AND STRAIGHTFORWARD PERSONALITY
Can deliver criticism and praise without personal prejudice. No 'edge'

CONSCIENTIOUS
Takes care over delivery of course and the boats and equipment

SENSITIVE
Adjusts delivery to suit individuals and takes interest in students

ENTHUSIASTIC
Own enjoyment of the sport is infectious even in adverse conditions such as no wind

RESPONSIBILITY
Understands responsibility for safety of students, stays in charge even when things go wrong

KNOWLEDGEABLE
Understands the subject and RYA scheme

PREPARING AND PRESENTING LESSONS ASHORE

TEACHING ASHORE

With small groups, much of the teaching is done informally around the boat or a portable board. With larger groups it is necessary to use some classroom teaching techniques. A lecture is not always the most effective way of teaching a practical subject like sailing. For example a bowline can only be taught by giving the students a rope and helping them to tie the knot. Merely stating a fact is no guarantee that your students will have received the information.

Bear the following points in mind when teaching:

- Before the first session welcome the students onto the course.
  An informal start helps you to find out who they are and their experience.

- Learn the students' names as soon as possible.

- Find out their experience: this will help you pitch the course at the right level.

- Consider the room layout.
  Anything you say or do will be pointless unless your students can see and hear you. Encourage your students to fill classrooms from the front. Make sure your room is comfortable, cool and well ventilated.

- Keep talks short.
  Twenty minutes is about the right length of lime to maintain students' attention without testing or a break. Don't over-run.

- Outline your aims at the beginning of a lesson and summarise the essential points to remember at the close.

- A handout stating the important facts is useful, but should not be given out until the end of the lecture. Handouts distributed at the beginning will only be read by students when they should be listening to you.

- Give your talk a structure:
  Introduction, Development, Summary, Test.

- Draw on practical examples to illustrate your points.
  Anecdotes should not be used to reinforce your personal brilliance - the class will quickly sense they are being taught by a knowledgeable and credible sailor, without you having to remind them regularly.

- Consider the age and experience of your audience (see notes on teaching adults).

- Technical language.
  Avoid complicated terms but define those which are essential. Before you answer questions on, say, sailing by the lee, ensure that the rest of the class know what you are talking about.

- Choose your position.
  Where and how you stand will have an effect on your talk. Standing behind a desk or lectern may appear more formal and puts a barrier between you and your audience.

Sitting on a table at the front of the class may be too relaxed for some talks. Watch polished speakers and assess their use of body language. Don't hide behind your visual aids.

- **Involve your students.**
  Speak to all of them. Don't talk to the ceiling, the floor or the wall at the back of the classroom. Try to make eye contact with every member of the audience at some stage. As alternatives to a monologue, use question and answer techniques, discussions etc and use students' names.

- **Avoid irritating mannerisms.**
  Your RYA instructor course will help to identify habits of which you may have no knowledge.

- **Avoid distractions.**
  Any distractions (e.g. Mannerisms) which take your students' attention away from what you are saying will damage your talk. If you are giving a talk outside because of good weather, arrange the group so that they are facing away from any distractions and such that the sun is in your eyes, not theirs.

- **Practise writing on blackboards and/or wipeboards.**
  Prepared overhead projector acetates are preferable to copious board-writing with your back to your students. Never talk to your board, always to your students. If you are not using or have finished with a board, rub it clean to avoid distraction.

Don't patronise the students

- **Don't bluff.**
  If you don't know the answer to a question - say so. Your students would far rather have an honest 'don't know, but I'll find out' than a bluffed answer. Having said that, you should always ensure that you have a wider knowledge of your subject than the basic facts contained in your lecture.

- **Don't be afraid to test.**
  Providing the questions are not threatening they can be used to maintain interest and will help to reinforce your teaching.

- **Avoid sarcasm, humiliation or rudeness.**
  Try not to let any of your prejudices alienate members of the class. In particular, avoid patronising students of a very different age group from your own and avoid sexism.

- Don't try to be funny unless you are naturally witty. The instructor course will help to appraise you of your natural level of humour.

Finally, remember that your talk will have succeeded only if all your students leave it having learnt all the important facts which you intended to communicate and are eager to learn more.

Teaching adults...

- Adults tend to have a greater fear of failure than children. They are therefore more reluctant to appear foolish in front of a class. You should concentrate on rewarding ideas and not on making those who give wrong answers feel inadequate. Adults will accept being corrected if it is done positively and is not humiliating.

- Adults for whom 'being lectured' is their only experience of being taught are initially reluctant to become involved in discussion, question and answer, tests and quizzes etc. Encourage them to ask questions and take part in the discussion. You will have to push against this dislike at first; once the students have overcome it they will learn more quickly and enjoy themselves more. Don't give anyone the opportunity to opt out. To encourage others, congratulate those who do join in initially.

- Adults are much more vulnerable to sarcasm than children, who tend to be used to it.

- The greater part of adult learning since leaving school will have been by 'problem solving' and personal experience. Use this to your advantage and let 'problem solving' from information you supply be one of your teaching methods, but remember that this approach usually takes longer than instructions.

- An adult's academic interest in the subject is not always compatible with his practical ability; the gap sometimes widens with age.

... and children

- Generally, young people make better students than adults, learning faster and with better retention.

- However, they are intolerant of poor classroom teaching. If their motivation is not high, it will be lowered further by a dull lecture in the classroom. Children learning within a group of relative strangers may initially be very shy about contributing answers. This in turn makes it difficult for the instructors to assess how much is being absorbed without resorting to testing, which again makes the process seem like school. Once you have overcome the shyness, you could find the opposite problem of having to control class input to the level which allows you to teach.

- Teaching young children (6-10) to sail requires a different approach to that for older children or adults. See the International Optimist Club Guide.

- Remember to explore the alternatives to the lecture: games ashore, work cards, modelling or drawing sessions.

- The Youth Sailing Scheme takes the different learning styles into account and is particularly suitable for young sailors. The initial training takes place in single handed dinghies (such as the Taz, Optimist and Pico) or suitable double handers (Pico Plus, Feva and Mirror).

PREPARATION AND USE OF VISUAL AIDS

We all communicate using a mixture of verbal and non-verbal information. A huge proportion of the message we transmit is tone of voice, eye contact, body language, etc. Good tuition requires the instructor or coach to make sure that they focus on keeping both types of message clear and inspirational.

Basic principles

• *Relevance*

Visual aids should be relevant or they become a distraction. Do not produce them for their own sake.

• *Clarity*

Diagrams must be simple and easily understood. They must be clearly read by the furthest of your audience. Any visual aid which cannot be seen by everyone is neither visual nor an aid.

• *Short slides*

Maximum four to six points per PowerPoint or OHP slide.

• *Timing*

Produce visual aids when needed; they will only distract your audience if displayed too soon. Dispose of them after use.

• *Display*

Try to display a visual aid in a dramatic manner. Students will remember something for longer if it is linked to a highlight.

• *Involvement*

A display of neatly tied knots on a board is much less effective than students attempting to tie the knots themselves, although the knotboard will be useful for reference after the lesson.

• *Use the other senses*

An aid which can be passed around, is more valuable than something which is merely displayed. Beware of moving on to another topic while your visual aid is still circulating. Nobody will listen to you if they have a toy with which to play. Equally, use the mechanism of some visual aids to 'punctuate' your lecture and put in 'paragraphs' i.e., switching off the OHP between acetates, lights on/off between slides.

• *Yourself*

Don't forget that you are a walking visual aid with optional sound yourself. Think about your mannerisms, delivery, position etc and their effect on the class. Never hide behind another visual aid such that your audience cannot see you properly. Finally, dress for the occasion. Although sailing is a practical sport, don't let your appearance serve as a distraction to your audience. A good general rule is to dress as well as the best dressed of your audience. You will then offend nobody.

Types of visual aid

It is often said that the best visual aid available to the sailing instructor is the boat itself, but the more advanced your teaching, the less true that statement becomes. Each of the other visual aids in common use has certain advantages and drawbacks.

Chalkboard or Wipeboard

These are widely available and can be portable. Be careful to talk to your students and not to the board. The disadvantages are that although adequate for simple messages or drawings it is unsatisfactory for detailed work to be done when the audience is present.

Flipchart

This has many of the characteristics of the chalkboard but the twin advantages that it is portable and information can be stored and used repeatedly.

Overhead projector

Properly used, this can be very versatile. Although it requires power, it can be used in daylight and without the instructor losing eye contact with the audience.

Although it is possible to write and draw as you speak, most instructors prefer to prepare OHP slides in advance. You can enhance them by the use of colour and by using overlays to build up or break down complex concepts or techniques.

Once a few operating tricks are learnt, the OHP is simple to use effectively but you must avoid the temptation to put too many words on an acetate. Remember that words are not visuals, even though they may be used to trigger thoughts or retain ideas. If you have a choice, position the screen in the corner of the room so that you are less likely to obstruct anyone's view.

Digital Projectors

These are becoming much more common although expensive. Slides and text can be produced on a PC using one of the many programmes now available. Avoid over-complication; an audience may be dazzled by the clever effects and miss the important messages of the presentation! Desktop or laptop computer simulations, often available from CD or the Internet, can be useful on certain courses.

Video or DVD films can be projected creating an ideal picture size for a larger audience. Computer generated and video films can be integrated.

The projector is also useful for compiling slide shows using stills from a digital camera.

KEEP AN ELEMENT OF EXCITEMENT IN YOUR COURSES...

Video

Either use professionally produced videos or a video camera afloat with your group. The RYA videos are intended to be used in sections, with the instructor interspersing the video with practical sessions. If using a video camera afloat consider the following:

Forget about the attractions of the zoom lens. Get as close to the action with as short a focal length as you can. The resulting picture will be far steadier and hence less likely to induce seasickness in the audience later.

Turn off the microphone. Even the professionals separate the roles of cameraman and commentator. Your 'off-the-cuff' comments are more likely to offend and be less helpful than a later commentary over a silent video.

Choose definite techniques or manoeuvres to film and switch off in between. Nothing is more aggravating for your students than having to sit through two hours of playback for the two minutes of their own sailing.

Models

Ranging from simple shapes used for collision avoidance talks to detailed models of sailing dinghies, the scope for models is limited only by the ability of the builder. In general, a model should have only enough detail as is required to ensure a full understanding of its role. Over-complication may be satisfying to the creator but must not detract from its use as a visual aid.

Land drills and shore-based demonstrations

Ideal for demonstrating complex skills at slow speed and without distraction. eg Tacks, gybes and spinnaker hoists/drops (see page 87).

AVOIDING COMPLAINTS

Most complaints arise from a lack of communication.

Students who have attended and passed the Level 2 course, often wish to take further modules, with virtually no further experience and without the ability to achieve the standard by the end of the course. Ideally the person taking the booking will spot this and either divert the student to a more suitable course or ensure that their aims are realistic. If not, the instructor has the job of redefining what can be achieved during the course. Someone who has paid for a course is expecting to receive the syllabus as defined in the logbook. The scheme is in modular form so that the appropriate training can be given to students who have a wide range of aptitudes and experiences.

Remember that the purpose of the scheme is to teach the sport and improve peoples' sailing. If the module is inappropriate the instructor should discuss realistic aims and ensure that the student agrees. A degree of tact and diplomacy is required to break this news but most people who have struggled on the first day will welcome a relief from the stress of trying to achieve an unrealistic target. Leave the possibility of the certificate open as people often improve once the pressure is off.

SO... YOU WANT TO COMPLAIN?

If you do not inform people of their progress you are more likely to receive a complaint along the lines of "I didn't achieve the certificate because I wasn't taught well".

Occasionally a student turns up who, for whatever reason, is likely to complain. If you can spot one of these, try to run the course exactly by the logbook, this handbook and your school's operating procedure. Before the end of the course, while there is still sailing time available, ask if they are satisfied with the course and if they would like to practise any further skills or techniques. Try to elicit regular feedback and give opportunities for comment.

The Principal or Chief Instructor should also give opportunities for feedback as the course progresses. We cannot expect every course to be perfect (equipment fails and the weather is unpredictable) but try to deliver the course to the best of your ability and to the guidelines of your school and the RYA. The students should then find the course worthwhile.

If a school receives a complaint the Principal or Chief Instructor should deal with it personally. Try to establish what the person complaining is asking for. An immediate and understandable reaction is 'How dare you criticise my centre' but a more helpful attitude is 'How can we resolve this?' Often the simplest option is to offer more tuition. If you can arrange this before they leave your centre, perhaps at a later date, you can save a lot of correspondence and bad feeling.

The instructors who receive the fewest complaints are those who are competent, take an interest in their students, and ensure that even the difficult or weak students feel they are an important part of the group. The instructional skills required are well beyond those of just sailing or even just teaching.

TEACHING DISABLED SAILORS

Teaching a disabled person to sail is exactly like teaching a non-disabled person. You mix common sense with experience and apply safe practice.

The overall objective is to learn how to sail effectively, develop confidence, enjoyment, a sense of achievement and to have fun. It is important to encourage maximum participation and activity by people. Do not prejudge a person's competence by their disability, but rather by their experience, knowledge and ability.

FOCUS ON PEOPLE'S ABILITIES - NOT DISABILITIES.

We are all individuals each with different interests. Someone with a disability has ideas, makes plans, gets excited, even bloody minded - in short they are just like the rest of us. There is no need to adopt a different manner and vocabulary or to feel sympathy or embarrassment. The important thing is to treat a disabled person as you would anyone else.

Communication is the key to success.

It is essential that communication is a two way process. Key points to remember are:

- Never assume
- Ask
- Listen
- Establish individual communication
- Emphasise the ability not disability

- Make the terminology/jargon clear
- Build trust
- Check understanding
- Offer empathy not sympathy
- Learn very basic sign language

A disability is not a barrier to the successful completion of courses. All participants must be able to demonstrate their ability to complete the whole syllabus, but this can be achieved by proxy. A candidate who cannot perform a task directly must be able to satisfactorily direct a third party to achieve that task on their behalf. It is worth bearing in mind that the candidate has to possess good communication and teaching skills as well as knowing how to undertake the manoeuvre.

The 'special endorsements' line of the certificate should be treated with care. Do not list any disability unless it directly affects the holder's ability to handle a boat, so the prosthesis that gives a user complete function is of no consequence. However, a visually impaired person may have the endorsement 'Requires visual assistance on the water'.

How RYA Sailability can support your training needs

Attitudes to the inclusion of disabled people in sport are forever changing, but we know that the biggest barriers of all are the concerns of non-disabled people. The barriers that these concerns create are often born of ignorance and apprehension, but most significantly from a lack of awareness.

Without the numerous club members and RYA Sailability Volunteers there would be no support to organise so many sailing opportunities throughout the country. As groups expand and new ones start up the demand for volunteers grows.

Disabled people want to go sailing and often need a variety of support to enable them to do so. Some are totally independent; others may need help with transport, launching boats etc. Volunteers do not have to be a sailor or paramedic to help someone get afloat, every job is important, but it is essential to identify what job is best for them.

RYA Sailability offers two training packages that can support your groups/clubs in both awareness and volunteer organisation.

RYA Sailability Awareness Training

A comprehensive training course that will allow and encourage helpers to become involved by alleviating their fear of disability and give them the knowledge needed to enjoy their involvement to the full. The course covers the following areas:

- The needs of sailors with disabilities, both ashore and afloat
- Improved communication skills
- The use of current terminology to explain disability
- The use of specialist equipment and adaptations
- Moving, handling and transfer techniques

At the end of the course all participants are given a booklet containing keynotes from the course and receive a course completion certificate, which can be pasted into the National Sailing Scheme Syllabus and Logbook G4.

Volunteers the Key to Success

This new five hour RYA Sailability Course is being promoted for all Sailability Clubs and has become a requirement for all clubs seeking Foundation Site status. This course differs significantly from other similar Volunteer Management Courses in that it includes the needs of Disabled People both from their need for volunteer support and also as volunteers in their own right. It includes how to recruit, manage, support and reward volunteers.

At the end of the course all participants are given a booklet containing keynotes from the course and are automatically registered with Sport England's "Valuing Volunteers Programme" from which they receive a number of valuable resources and regular updates. They also receive a course completion certificate, which can be pasted into the National Sailing Scheme Syllabus and Logbook G4.

Courses are held throughout the UK, to find out about your nearest course please contact RYA Sailability 0845 3450403.

I THOUGHT THEY WERE SUPPOSED TO BE SLOW...!

ASSESSING YOUR STUDENTS' ABILITIES

Youth Sailing Scheme

The syllabi for each of the stages of the Start Sailing and Advanced Sailing Awards are clearly expressed in terms of competencies. As the student is able to do each item, so it can be signed off. When all the items for a particular award are complete, the certificate or sticker may be given. On any course, it is possible that some students will complete some extra items from the next stages, in which case those items can also be signed off.

National Sailing Scheme

The aim of the National Sailing Scheme is to introduce and promote different aspects of the sport in an enjoyable, safe and informative manner. It exists to give people the skills and confidence they need to pursue their chosen path in the sport. It is much more important that the students enjoy their time afloat and improve their skills, than that the highest possible certification standards are set.

By the end of the course students should have achieved a practical understanding of the material, but may still be making mistakes. Such a student may be awarded a certificate. A student who has just reached the standard will typically use the correct techniques (eg close reaching towards the jetty), but their manoeuvres will not always succeed (eg stopping short, backing the jib and tacking off).

On the other hand, a student who uses incorrect techniques (eg gybing a GP14 with the centreboard down and the main in during a Performance Sailing course) has probably not reached the correct standard.

A successful student who should receive a certificate will be one who is approaching the course material in the right way, but may require further practice to succeed consistently.

Level 1 Start Sailing

The aim of the Adults Level 1 course is to get people afloat in a relaxed, enjoyable manner. The emphasis is on practical teaching techniques. To gain the Level 1 certificate, the student simply has to demonstrate each of those techniques whilst being taught.

Level 2 Basic Skills

If your student can rig and launch a boat, sail around a triangular course, come alongside or pick up a mooring or man overboard and then return safely to shore, he is competent to Level 2.

You are not concerned with perfect sail setting or boat handling, but will look for an appreciation of the five essentials and a successful negotiation of the course. You should do as much of the assessment as possible on a continuous basis, entering items in the logbook as they are completed to avoid 'exam nerves'.

Many centres conduct the final assessment in a tactful way, by treating the triangular course sessions as informal races. The syllabus therefore contains the minimum which the candidate needs to know for success on this exercise.

The aim at this level is to encourage students to continue sailing and go further in the scheme, so the certificate is awarded unless the student cannot manage the objective assessment above or is actively dangerous. Adults generally prefer oral interviews to written papers for the assessment of background knowledge.

Seamanship Skills

By this stage, the student is expected not only to negotiate a triangular course, but to sail in moderate winds. The 5 essentials may not be applied correctly all the time but this should not be fundamentally affecting boat control so that safety is affected or control is lost.

It is not essential that all of the sailing techniques and manoeuvres are completed totally successfully first time, but the student must understand what he should have done, why he failed and be successful on at least some attempts.

Some training centres have theory papers to help with assessments. If you are asked to assess one of these, study the paper to familiarise yourself with the depth of knowledge required and ensure that you know all the answers.

Day Sailing

On completion of the course the successful sailor will have a confident, safe approach to planning and executing a short cruise in a dinghy/keelboat/multihull.

The course will include the planning and execution of a short cruise, giving candidates an opportunity to experiment with the material and show that they have understood it. While it may not be possible to cover the entire syllabus in a practical way, subjects such as boat handling and decision making in deteriorating conditions should be thoroughly discussed either afloat or ashore.

Sailing with Spinnakers

On completion of the course the successful sailor will understand how to rig, launch and sail a dinghy/keelboat/multihull rigged with an asymmetric or symmetric spinnaker.

Depending on the equipment available and the interests of the students, the course may include symmetric, asymmetric or both types of spinnaker. Once the basics have been mastered, the instructor should concentrate on coaching the students to improve their performance.

Start Racing

This course is designed to give the confidence, skills and knowledge needed to take part in club racing in good conditions. Confidence is essential if the sailor is to enjoy racing. The course involves the sailor in a variety of enjoyable exercises designed to build confidence and improve skills through practice.

While some shore-based teaching is unavoidable, this course is essentially a practical one and should be delivered primarily through short practical workshops.

The successful sailor will be aware of his basic obligations to others and able to control his boat around the course.

Performance Sailing

On completion of this course the successful sailor will understand how to sail performance dinghies/keelboats/multihulls to best advantage at all times. They will have an understanding of how to set up and handle the boat in a variety of wind conditions and demonstrate a degree of sensitivity to the boat in applying the 5 essentials.

The emphasis is on coaching to improve the candidate's sailing performance. This will involve coaching from powerboats.

The course is intended primarily for two-person spinnaker boats. However it may be delivered in performance single-handers and the certificate endorsed accordingly.

MANUAL HANDLING

Manual handling is any transporting or supporting of a load (including the lifting, putting down, pushing, pulling carrying or moving thereof) by hand or bodily force.

As an Instructor it is worth being aware that workplace injuries can affect your life and recreation as well as your work, particularly in later years. Injuries sustained while sailing can also affect your students.

This includes sudden injuries in the workplace as well as cumulative wear and tear, commonly caused by poor positioning over a period of time.

Common risks arise from:

- Excessive or awkward loads for one person

- Slippery or uneven surfaces

- Repetition or excessive duration of tasks

Slipways, jetties and dragging boats can all give rise to these circumstances. Studies show that the overwhelming proportion of accidents in the workplace are sprains or strains due to manual handling. Of these, back injuries are three times more common than any other injury.

The Manual Handling Operations Regulations 1992 contain guidance suggesting that manual handling should be included in risk assessments and that employers, employees and volunteers should take sensible steps to minimise the risks.

TOP TIP

Five handling tips for instructors

1 Widen the base of support whilst lifting/carrying

2 Keep the load inside the base of support whenever possible

3 Avoid asymmetry, eg carrying a heavy fuel can

4 In general before lifting:
   ASSESS: task, load, environment, individual(s)
   PLAN: task, route
   PREPARE: load, self, area

5 Lift using the six point lift:

- Look at the load
- Bend knees/straight back
- Lift with legs/load close
- Foot position
- Test the load/firm grip
- Put down with care

ENVIRONMENTAL ISSUES

Dinghy sailing can be a very environmentally friendly sport - after all, we mainly use wind power - a renewable form of energy. However, because of the growing popularity of water sports, there is increasing concern about the potential damage that could occur to our valuable wetland and coastal environments if we, and other boat users, behave irresponsibly. Whilst we all want to encourage our sport, it is essential that we take very seriously the need to protect the environment and ensure quality of life now and for generations to come. This is known as Sustainable Development. For dinghy sailors, and all those who enjoy the coast and inland lakes and waterways, this includes paying particular attention to disposal of waste, pollution, the protection of wildlife, habitats and other natural features, and consideration for other water users.

Here are a few guidelines for dinghy sailors and their crews to reduce harmful impacts:

The Sailing area

- Find out if there are any particularly sensitive areas such as Nature Reserves. It is also possible that the site is legally designated for its nature conservation importance, where exceptional care is required. See 'Wildlife & the Law',

- Take particular care to avoid disturbance to nesting birds between March and July; vulnerable habitats are salt marshes, some shingle beaches, sand dunes, reedbeds, and islands within inland lakes and lochs. Avoid landing on these areas and sailing nearby with noisy crews!

- Only use official landing and launching sites to avoid erosion of bank and shore vegetation.

- Avoid regular anchoring within sea grass beds (Zostera). This is an important and fragile habitat.

Motorised craft

Rescue craft need to respond quickly, but 'the need for speed' has an environmental impact!

- Reduce bank erosion by keeping speeding limits and avoiding excess wash.

- Use 4-stroke engines if possible. Two-stroke motors are less efficient and can discharge more toxic chemicals through exhaust emissions.

- Keep away from vulnerable habitats (see above) particularly during the bird nesting season.

- Take particular care to avoid water pollution while refuelling, especially afloat.

- Respect other water users; reduce speed and noise.

Boat Maintenance

Most modern dinghies are made of plastic or composite materials. Repairs often require the use of oil-based paints, solvents and other potentially hazardous substances.

- Carefully dispose of all paint and solvent containers after-use. Follow directions on the labels.

- Maintain and check all fuel lines, connections and seals in good condition.

Good environmental practice for boat users

- Antifouling paints, even in small doses, can be extremely toxic to wildlife. Ensure old paint scrapings do not get swept into the water. Avoid spillages when painting.
- When replacing wood, use timber from well managed, sustainable, forests e.g. certified by the Forest Stewardship Council. The harvesting of some tropical hardwoods can result in considerable damage to rain forests.
- Remember to turn the light off in the workshop when not in use!

Rubbish

We all produce rubbish, bottles, cans and waste from packed lunches, old equipment rope and twine and rubbish from boat maintenance. Do not throw it overboard:

Refuse repair or recycle

- Refuse - do you really need that extra gadget!
- Repair and re-use - support boat jumbles - someone might be looking for that discontinued line or special part.
- Recycle. Instead of throwing away old aluminium parts in general waste: give them to metal scrap dealers - you may get some money back!

When disposing of waste, separate materials and use different bins provided: metals, bottles, even Wellington boots! Old batteries from motorised craft should be disposed of at a dedicated reception facility at the local waste collection site

Good Practice

Many busy waterways, both inland and on the coast, now have management plans to avoid conflicting interests. As a senior member of a sailing club or school, you may be asked to represent your organisation on a management committee. There will be opportunities to put your point of view and listen to other groups. If we work together and learn from each other we shall continue to enjoy our activities and help minimise environmental impact.

Useful Contacts

English Nature   www.english-nature.org.uk
Northminster House, Peterborough, PE1 1UA

Environment Agency   www.environment-agency.gov.uk
Rio House, Waterside Drive, Aztec west, Almondsbury, Bristol, BS12 4UD

British Marine Industries Federation   www.bmif.co.uk (follow 'Environment' link)

Countryside Council for Wales   www.ccw.gov.uk

Marine Conservation Society   www.mcsuk.org.uk
9 Gloucester Road, Ross-on-Wye, Herefordshire HR9 5BU

Joint Nature Conservation Committee(JNCC) Monkstone House, City Road, Peterborough PE1 1JY www.jncc.gov.uk

Royal Society for Nature Conservation (RSNC),
The Wildlife Trusts Partnership   www.rsnc.org.uk
22 The Green, Witham Park, Waterside South, Lincoln LN5 7JR

Royal Society for the Protection of Birds   www.rspb.org.uk
The Lodge, Sandy, Bedfordshire SG19 2DL

Scottish Natural Heritage   www.snh.gov.uk
12 Hope Terrace, Edinburgh EH9 2AS

Wildlife & the Law

Wildlife in many inland and coastal sailing areas is now safeguarded under national and international laws to ensure protection against potentially damaging activities and operations. Importantly, not all of these sites will be signposted as 'Nature Reserves'. Familiarise yourself with the following designations and find out if any apply to your area:

SSSI - Site of Special Scientific Interest

Designated in the United Kingdom by English Nature, Scottish Natural Heritage and Countryside Council for Wales. Potentially damaging operations (PDOs) might include the construction of slipways, seawalls and habitat damage and disturbance.

EC Habitats Directive

Designated habitats are known as Special Areas of Conservation (SACs). www.jncc.gov.uk/SACselection

EC Birds Directive   Sites designated are known as Special Protection Areas (SPAs). www.jncc.gov.uk/idt/SPA

Ramsar Sites

Waterfowl (wild ducks and geese) are protected under the international Ramsar Convention. www.jncc.gov.uk/idt/ramsar

Remember, that as a dinghy sailor, you can help guard and protect our precious waterways by reporting any pollution incidents immediately to the Environment Agency. The local Wildlife Trust should be informed of any sightings of rare or unusual wildlife.

INSTRUCTOR TRAINING COURSES

ASSISTANT INSTRUCTOR TRAINING

The role of the Assistant Instructor is to assist qualified instructors to teach beginners up to the standard of the National Sailing Certificate, Level 2 Basic Skills, and Start Sailing Stages 1, 2 and 3 of the Youth Sailing Scheme. It follows that the training given should cover the teaching points related to teaching beginners, in the sections starting on pages 50 and 67 of this book.

This training may either be given on a specific Assistant Instructor course over about 20 hours, or may be provided on a one-to-one basis over a longer period as on-the-job training. A suggested programme for a weekend course is given below, the majority of the time being spent afloat covering how to put across the various teaching points for each of the method sessions.

As this training is related directly to the work of a single training centre, it follows that the emphasis is likely to be predominantly either on double handed or single handed dinghies. In providing this training, the Principal or Chief Instructor will have in his mind the role of the Assistant Instructor - helping qualified RYA Instructors. In double handed boats, the Assistant Instructor may act as helmsman in the very early stages of training, and then encourage the students to take over as soon as possible.

When teaching in single handers the Assistant Instructor's role is often that of helper, rigger, catcher, etc. The training given will reflect this.

Following training, candidates will be assessed on their practical teaching ability with beginners, according to the criteria given under Instructor Assessment in this Handbook.

Sample programme for Assistant Instructor course		
Friday	evening	Welcome, Introductions, role of the Assistant Instructor Outline of course Basic principles of instructor technique
Saturday	morning afternoon evening	Teaching method sessions 1-4 Teaching method sessions 5-7 Teaching capsize recovery and man overboard (theory)
Sunday	morning afternoon	Teaching method sessions 8-11 Teaching method session 12 Teaching capsize recovery and man overboard (practical) Debrief

THE INSTRUCTOR PRE-ENTRY SAILING ASSESSMENT

In order to be accepted for training at instructor level all candidates have to pass a practical test conducted by an RYA Coach/Assessor, not more than one year before instructor training. The test serves as a filter, because there is no time during the instructor course for candidates to be taught how to sail well.

It is recommended that, prior to taking the assessment, candidates satisfy themselves that they can sail a dinghy confidently to the standard detailed below and have the appropriate background knowledge.

During the assessment, which will normally be conducted in a minimum wind speed of 11 knots by an RYA Coach/Assessor, the candidate will be judged on his preparation for and execution of each of the tasks, including awareness of others. The assessment will be made in a boat of the candidate's choice with a Portsmouth Yardstick of less than 1230. If the assessment is conducted in a keelboat or multihull the rudderless sailing section should be omitted.

The assessment may be undertaken during a course run by an RYA Coach/Assessor. Candidates for a coastal instructor certificate should undertake the sailing assessment on coastal waters.

The candidate should be able to complete the following tasks, sailing at all times with an awareness of 'the Five Essentials' i.e. sail setting, balance, trim, centreboard and course sailed. The Assessor will be seeking to confirm that you can sail competently and confidently, by completing the following exercises.

You will always be asked to complete the following

1 Sail around a triangular course

- Each leg of the course will be a minimum of 100 metres

- Use the five essentials

- Close mark rounding

- Allow for tide if appropriate

- Use all the boat's equipment to best advantage including spinnaker if carried.

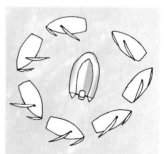

2 Sail a tight circular course

- Circle less than three boat lengths' radius around a stationary (free floating) boat

- Make only one tack and one gybe

- Sail trim and boat balance/trim suited to the manoeuvre.

The circle should be as small as you can safely make it, but the Assessor will accept that, in doing, this, you might have to leave the centreboard in one position.

3 Sail a follow-my-leader course

The course may include all points of sailing and may be behind another sailing dinghy or behind a powered boat. The Assessor will be looking for a small, constantly maintained distance between you and the boat ahead on all points of sailing. A boat length or less is usual.

4 Pick up a man overboard dummy

- Boat must be stopped dead in the water when you pick up the dummy

- Pick up at the windward shroud
- Do not tack while you pull it aboard
- More than one attempt should not be needed

You may also be asked to complete some of the following:

1.Sail without a rudder, or with the tiller on a loose elastic

This exercise highlights your appreciation of the five essentials and demonstrates whether you understand the effects of variations in sail trim and boat balance/trim.

The Assessor may ask you to sail around a triangular course with the tiller loosely secured using an elastic loop, or with the rudder raised or removed. You will be expected to make good progress around the course in a seamanlike manner.

He will expect you to make any modifications to sail area, sheeting arrangements and centreboard position before you start, so that the whole exercise proceeds smoothly. You will not be penalised for reefing the dinghy, if conditions are such that it would be seamanlike to do so. In the unlikely event of there being several boats sailing rudderless in any area, the Assessor would expect you to maintain good awareness of the other boats and take avoiding action early if necessary.

2 Lee shore landing and departure

- Use correct sail plan (jib only if necessary)
- Land in a controlled fashion
- On departure clear the shore successfully in a controlled way on the first attempt

3 Anchor or pick up a mooring - wind against tide (if appropriate)

- Correct sail plan
- Boat should be stopped dead next to the buoy
- Pick up buoy first time
- When mooring buoy is on board, the boat should remain under your control
- Anchoring to take place in the area designated by the Assessor
- Anchoring should be successful on the first attempt
- After the anchor has held, the boat should remain under your control

4 Come alongside a moored boat, wind against tide (if appropriate)

- Approach under control
- Stop alongside on the first attempt
- Remain in control thereafter

The choice of exercises above allows for pre-entry assessments being carried out in different locations and different conditions. The decision as to which ones are used will be made by the Assessor, who will be judging your preparation and execution of the task, including the fact that you have an escape route planned.

Throughout this section the phrase 'on the first attempt' should not be taken to mean that you cannot make a seamanlike decision to break off at a reasonably early stage and try again. It merely means that once you have become committed to a task, it should be successfully completed.

5 Recover a capsized dinghy and sail away

You should successfully right your boat, without external help, in a calm and controlled fashion. Except in the case of gear failure you should need only one attempt. Do be prepared for this task by checking the boat (loose gear, buoyancy etc) and yourself (clothing, personal buoyancy) before the event.

Throughout the pre-entry sailing assessment, the Assessor will try to obtain an overall impression of your sailing ability. As a result, you might technically fail one task and still pass the assessment if he feels you are up to the overall standard required of an RYA Instructor.

Just as you would not approach the driving test in a strange car without having practised reversing into a narrow opening etc, so you should not attempt the pre-entry assessment without practising all the tasks in the boat in which you intend to take the test.

Finally, please remember that although the pre-entry is likely to be conducted in a double-handed dinghy, the instructor course will include practical work in single handlers. All instructors are therefore expected to be capable of sailing the single-handers commonly used within training centres such as Optimists, Picos, Toppers and Lasers. Any Instructor candidate unfamiliar with these boats is recommended to gain some experience of them before the Instructor training course.

THE INSTRUCTOR TRAINING COURSE

Throughout your training it is important to remember that the RYA teaching methods used have been developed successfully over many years. You will be introduced to some techniques which have become standardised because it is important that RYA instruction should follow broadly the same pattern in every training centre.

It is equally important, however, that you should not follow certain drills slavishly without considering in more general terms the task which you are trying to accomplish. Without scope for minor variations, there would be no room for development and improvement.

TEACHING BEGINNERS - LEVELS 1 AND 2

Whilst there are agreed methods for teaching virtually every aspect of our sport, the part of teaching which has become widely known as 'The Method' covers the practical techniques of basic boat handling in the Start Sailing course, Level 1.

Although this course is used on its own as a short 'taster' by many training centres, it also forms the first two days of the conventional four or five day beginners' course leading to the award of the Basic Skills certificate, Level 2. This is the backbone of training provided by almost every centre.

The standardised teaching techniques enable Instructors to move from one centre to another and teach any part of the appropriate RYA course. Students can follow a course at one centre with a higher level course elsewhere, and the Instructors will know exactly what has been covered and what needs to be taught next.

The Method analyses the various elements that make up the activity of sailing a small boat, splitting each element into simple stages. Emphasis is placed on revision and testing to ensure that each stage has been successfully learnt.

It is important for motivation that students succeed at each stage, so the pace of learning and the complexity of the task are adapted to the individual. Students are encouraged to work out solutions from basic premises supplied by the instructor. In educational terms, it is a student-centred method based on experiential learning. When teaching beginners, different centres may use slightly different variations of the Method but all retain the basic philosophy. Thus the RYA Instructor should find no difficulty in adapting to local differences or 'house rules' within the basic framework.

The instructor course concentrates on the detail of the Method but you must never forget the overall aim - to get students sailing safely on their own as soon as possible. Each skill is broken down into easy steps for learning but, once learnt, those steps should disappear again as the manoeuvre becomes a continuous flowing action.

A student who, having mastered a technique, then adapts what he has been taught to suit himself should never be criticised because he has departed from the Method for that technique. He should be encouraged to move on and learn more.

The following outline of the Teaching Method provides the sequence of sessions and the important teaching points. Your course will expand on this framework. When actually using the Method to teach beginners, some sessions may well be run together, but it is worth establishing the principle that after only 20 minutes or so the average student's ability to absorb information falls off considerably. A short break, followed by revision and informal testing, makes for much more efficient learning.

Early in your own training you will realise that the Method avoids technical terminology. 'Ropes, seats, push and pull' are preferable to instructions which are complicated by unfamiliar terms. Your students will be having enough trouble working out what is going on without being told to 'sheet out and bear away'. Some nautical terms in common use come so naturally, however, that they will almost certainly be learnt in the first sessions.

FLOW DIAGRAM FOR TEACHING METHOD

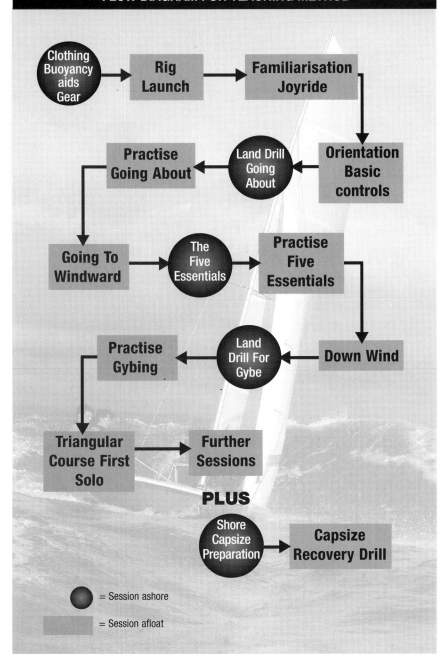

Clothing Buoyancy aids Gear → Rig Launch → Familiarisation Joyride

Practise Going About ← Land Drill Going About ← Orientation Basic controls

Going To Windward → The Five Essentials → Practise Five Essentials

Practise Gybing ← Land Drill For Gybe ← Down Wind

Triangular Course First Solo → Further Sessions

PLUS

Shore Capsize Preparation → Capsize Recovery Drill

● = Session ashore

■ = Session afloat

Session 1 Ashore
Clothing/Footwear/Buoyancy aids/Gear collection

- Warm clothing: wetsuit, dry suit, waterproofs
- Footwear: Wellies, trainers or sailing shoes
- Buoyancy aid: 50 Newtons, correct size, securely fastened, 150 Newtons life jackets for non-swimmers
- Gear collection: identify each item briefly

Session 2 Ashore or Afloat
Rigging/Launching

Rigging

- Rig boat quickly
- Involve students
- Explain briefly
- Reef if necessary

Launching and underway

- Don't waste time
- Hoist main
- Ask students and indicate wind direction

TOP TIP

Cold people don't learn and quickly become unsafe.

Wet clothes speed up cooling.

Keep your students as dry as possible

Session 3 Afloat
Familiarisation/Joyride

Do not be in too much of a hurry to start instruction but give your students time to absorb the sensation of being in a sailing boat perhaps for the first time. They should be looking out of the dinghy and not inside, enjoying the new sensation of being afloat. The joyride also demonstrates your skill and, by making no demands of your students, allows everyone to relax.

- Interesting, enthusiastic and enjoyable
- Instructor at helm
- Students allocated tasks
- Students balance boat and gain awareness of wind direction
- Short session
- Calm, relaxed and controlled
- Return to shore

TOP TIP

Learn about obvious landmarks so you can point them out to students in an interesting way

Session 4 Afloat
Orientation/Basic Boat Control

Orientation

- Point out landmarks and wind direction (particularly after manoeuvres such as tacking)
- Lying-to
- Figure of eight course with tack at each end
- Students take helm with target to aim at

- Instructor sits to leeward and forward of the helmsman
- Hands off the tiller
- Simple instructions such as 'pull it towards you a little'

Demonstrate basic boat controls:

- From lying-to position pull mainsail to turn boat towards wind
- Pull jib in to turn away from wind
- Relate changes in boat direction to the direction of the wind
- Students practise
- Discreetly moving your weight may be necessary to guarantee success
- Effect of raising centreboard
- No-go-zone (the windward sector in which the sails flap)

Session 5 Afloat and Ashore
Tacking or Going About

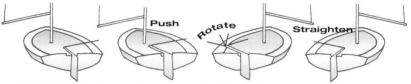
Push | Rotate | Straighten

Whether the dinghy is centre or aft mainsheet rigged the process is still the same

This is the first complicated manoeuvre your students will attempt. The learning can be divided into three sections:

A. The very basic skill of turning into the wind through 180°

B. The skill (developed later) of tacking through 90° while sailing to windward

C. Hints and tips for different situations.

A. The basics - turning into the wind through 180°

- Not all students will require a land drill, which is best done on a boat ashore
- Demonstrate at normal speed

The process is as follows:

1. At the start of the manoeuvre the dinghy should be flat.
2. If the sheeting arrangement is from the transom the helmsman changes hands (extension and mainsheet).
3. The turn is initiated by easing the tiller extension smoothly away.
4. As boom nears centreline, helmsman starts to move across boat, facing forwards if the boat is centre main rigged or aft if transom rigged.
5. Helmsman revolves extension away from him forward of tiller.*

* If the extension is too long to pass between the end of the tiller and the centre falls it will have to be swung towards the stern and over the tiller. This is done by sliding the hand down the extension, swivelling it around, and sliding the hand back to the end.

6. As boom reaches new leeward quarter helmsman sits down.

7. Helmsman centralises tiller as boat points towards new target and mainsail fills.

8. If the dinghy is centre-mainsheet rigged he changes hands at this point by bringing the sheet hand back across in front of his body to hold both tiller extension and sheet. He takes mainsheet with his front hand and brings extension under arm to front of body.

Teaching the basics of tacking through the wind

Very few students will absorb all the information listed above in one go. Teach the skills a little at a time, progressively adding bits in. A 'teaching summary' might therefore be:

Before turning

- •.Check the area to windward
- •.Warn your crew

Then

1 Ease the tiller away from you, towards the sail

2 As the dinghy turns under the boom, begin to move across to the other side

3 Extend the tiller arm

4 Sit down on the new side

5 As the sail fills straighten the tiller

Whether the dinghy is centre or aft mainsheet rigged the basic process is the same.

Choose obvious targets for students to sail towards after tacking

Notes

- At the start of the manoeuvre the dinghy should be flat
- If you are tacking a centre mainsheet dinghy change hands when the tack is complete Face basically forward during the manoeuvre
- If you are tacking an aft mainsheet dinghy change hands before you push the tiller away. Face aft during the manoeuvre
- In some dinghies the tiller extension may have to be rotated over the transom

During the learning period the instructor will be in full control of the dinghy, instructing the crew and choosing the appropriate time and place to turn. Once the process is mastered the instructor can pass control over to the student.

The student helmsman will then have to:

- Decide when it is appropriate to tack
- Check area into which he is going to sail
- Warn the crew by calling 'Ready about'
- As he eases the tiller extension firmly away call 'Lee oh'

Train the crew to take the following action as the dinghy is turned:

- When the helmsman calls 'Ready about' the crew uncleats jib sheet and checks area
- When he is ready, he answers 'Yes' to the call 'Ready about'
- As the boom reaches the centreline crew takes up slack in new jib sheet and moves across boat
- As the mainsail fills crew sheets in jib

B. Tacking through 90° - the complete manoeuvre

The Teaching Points (not the script) of the full 90° tacking manoeuvre are as follows:

Tacking Aft Mainsheet	Tacking Centre Mainsheet
• Helmsman faces aft and uses frying pan grip (palm up thumb on top)	• Helmsman faces forward throughout and uses dagger grip
• Spare mainsheet towards stern under the tiller	• Helmsman checks area into which he is going to sail
• Boat flat	• If clear, calls 'Ready about'
• Front hand holds mainsheet	• Crew uncleats jib sheet and checks area.
• Helmsman checks area into which he is about to sail	• When ready, he answers 'Yes'
• Helmsman says 'Ready About'	• Helmsman eases mainsheet slightly and calls ' Lee oh' as he eases the tiller extension away
• Crew checks and, if clear, answers 'Yes'	• As the boom reaches the centreline, he moves into the boat, back foot first, facing forward
• Helmsman changes hands on mainsheet and tiller extension by trapping the mainsheet under thumb of rear hand and picking up tiller extension in front hand	• Crew starts to move across
• Initiates turn by easing tiller extension smoothly away from him, saying 'Lee oh' as he does it	• Helmsman revolves extension around forward of tiller, moving across boat and still holding mainsheet in old front hand
• As boom reaches leeward quarter, crew releases jib sheet	• Crew takes up slack in new jib sheet and moves across boat
• As boom nears centreline, helmsman starts to move across boat, facing aft and moving his front foot first	• As sails fill, helmsman sits down on new side, steering with tiller arm behind back
• Helmsman revolves extension away from him forward of tiller	• He centralises the tiller as the sail fills, and brings sheet hand back across in front of body to hold both tiller extension and sheet, thumb pointing towards end of tiller extension. He takes mainsheet with his front hand and brings extension under arm to front of body
• Crew picks up new jib sheet and balances boat.	
• As boom reaches new leeward quarter, both helmsman and crew sit down	• Crew sheets in jib
• Helmsman centralises the tiller as the sail fills	• Continue to practise until instruction not required.
• Crew sheets in jib.	

A common fault is to sit down too far back after the tack, thus restricting the amount of room available for the tiller. Make sure your students sit as far forward as possible after the tack.

C. Variations on the Method - different situations

There are several variations for centre mainsheet boats in addition to the basic one outlined above. Which one is appropriate does depend to some extent on the boat and its equipment.

A common problem is where the length of the tiller extension makes bringing the extension under the arm difficult (eg a large adult in a Pico):

• Once settled on the new tack, steering with the front arm behind one's back, bring the sheet hand across in front of the body to hold tiller extension and sheet as before, but point the thumb <u>away</u> from the end of the extension (frying pan grip).

• Take the mainsheet with your front hand as normal.

- Finally rotate the extension <u>over</u> the arm and in front of the body, changing to dagger grip as you do so.

Many modern boats have such long tiller extensions that the tiller extension will not fit past the mainsheet falls (eg RS400), though this is easier if the student crosses the boat after the boom has moved across. In this case simply slide your tiller hand down the extension as you come into the boat (preventing over-steering) and rotate the extension around the back of the boat over the transom. After crossing the boat, proceed using one of the methods above.

Session 6 Afloat
Tacking Practice

After practice the student should be able to sail around a shallow figure of eight course, going about at each end, without any help from the Instructor. Don't forget to revise and to test at the beginning of the session.

- Tack from reach to reach often
- Ensure boat is going fast enough to tack
- Check crew and jib position
- Repeat shore drill if necessary
- Remember that good tacking is based on balance and foot placement

It is important that 'The Method' for tacking and gybing can lead to progressive improvement and refinement. For example, students who step across too soon will be unable to roll tack (allowing the boat to roll over and the boom to cross fully before crossing the boat) at a later stage.

Session 7 Afloat
Going to Windward

In fluctuating winds, sailing on a close reach initially will make life easier for your students. Be careful about wind shifts.

- Demonstrate that the sails flap as boat turns towards the wind
- Demonstrate the No-go-zone again
- Demonstrate and explain the concept of beating to windward
- Take the boat downwind
- Hand over to the student and ask to be sailed to a point directly upwind

Many students will now be able to do this unaided so only intervene if you feel that it is really necessary.

- Don't worry if the tacking is inefficient
- Use the flapping of the jib luff as an indicator of the edge of the No-go-zone
- Relate progress to landmarks
- Check ability to determine wind direction
- Stress that the angle between the sails and the wind stays the same wherever the boat is pointing.

TOP TIP

Sticking to a clear script helps a great deal as students try to build on the essentials. A typical script for the helmsman of a modern centre mainsheet dinghy might be "Stand up. Hand up. Straighten up"

- Wait for the boom to cross the centre-line of the boat, then:
- Stand and step across the boat back foot first (Stand Up)
- Raise tiller hand until extension is vertical (Hand Up)
- Centralise tiller to stop the turn (Straighten Up)

Tacking will now be through 90° although the novice may tack from close reach to close reach initially. Therefore a more progressive tack will replace the 180° turn.

- Ensure the boat is flat
- Crew bring their weight inboard to initiate turn
- The dinghy will turn towards the wind as it heels
- Steer through the wind but discourage over-steering
- Crew's feet are brought under the body as the dinghy turns
- The mainsail is eased
- Helm and crew move across together
- The dinghy is brought upright and the mainsail sheeted in

TOP TIP

The Five Essentials should form a continuous thread at every level. Comment on all five whatever the theme of the session.

Session 8 Ashore and Afloat
The Five Essentials
The five essentials contain the core skills required to sail a boat properly

1 Sail Setting

- Restate the point regarding the angle between the sails and the wind
- Simple board sketch or a working model
- Sails should be 'just not flapping'. Ease sails when turning away from the wind and sheet in when turning towards the wind (which will also aid tacking)
- One of the most common faults at this stage is the failure to sheet out when bearing away.

2 Balance

- Sail upright for minimum drag
- Demonstrate afloat how heeling makes the boat turn
- Every rudder movement slows the boat
- Remember 'Balance affects turning'

3 Boat Trim

- Show trim for different points of sailing. Explain why the boat goes better close hauled with weight forward
- Remember 'Trim affects speed'

TOP TIP

When sailing to windward, the action of the jib signals the wind direction.

4 Centreboard

- Demonstrate settings for different points of sailing

5 Course Sailed

- Explain different courses that will take you to windward. If the students are ready, introduce the idea that one course may be better than another because of tide, wind shadows or hazards - all in a very basic form
- Encourage students to make their own decisions based on personal observation.

Session 9 Afloat
Downwind

- Revise and test all previous work

- Concentrate on the training run

- Demonstrate the action of the jib as the training run turns into a dead run

- Allow plenty of room (wind against tide is ideal)

- Students practise running, turning from a beam reach, through a broad reach to a training run and then back to close-hauled

- Any change in direction requires changes in the Five Essentials

- Avoid gybing but also avoid horror stories about it

- End this session with a smooth controlled demonstration gybe

TOP TIP

Sailing downwind, the action of the jib gives a clear indication of wind direction and shifts (by the lee, dead run, training run.)

Session 10 Afloat and Ashore

Gybing

Similar to tacking, learning the manoeuvre can be divided into three sections:

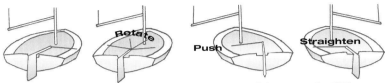

Whether the dinghy is centre or aft mainsheet rigged the process is still the same

A. The basic skill of turning through the gybe

B. The full manoeuvre

C. Hints and tips for different situations

Shore Drills for Gybing

- Explain fundamental difference between tacking and gybing

- Take the fear out of gybing

- Stress the very clear difference in commands – 'Ready About' for tacking but 'Stand by to Gybe' for gybing which avoids any possible confusion

- Concentrate on smooth and inspiring actions

- During any land drill, what you <u>do</u> is more important than what you <u>say</u>

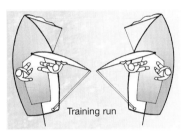

Training run

A The basic process for gybing is as follows

1 Helmsman sits forward of the tiller and puts the boat on a training run (jib action)

2 Centreboard is only slightly down

3 Helmsman pulls in mainsheet to bring boom clear of shroud

4 If the sheeting arrangement is from the transom the helmsman changes hands (extension and mainsheet) and moves towards middle of boat facing backwards taking the tiller extension round and forward towards the other side. If the dinghy is centre-main rigged he faces forwards as he moves to the centre, but does not change hands

5. The extension swings right around the end of the tiller without the tiller itself being moved

6 In an aft-rigged dinghy the helmsman initiates gybe by smoothly pushing the tiller extension towards where he was sitting and waits for the boom to swing across. If centre main rigged the helmsman also uses the falls of the mainsheet to bring the boom across positively at the right moment

7 As the mainsail clew lifts, the helmsman quickly centralises the tiller so that his weight, the boom and the tiller are simultaneously in the middle of the boat

8 He sits out on the new windward side

9 If centre main he changes hands as outlined in the tacking section

Teaching turning away from the wind – Gybing

As with tacking, very few students will absorb all the information listed above in one go. It is necessary to teach the skills a little at a time, progressively adding bits in. A 'teaching summary' might therefore be:

Before turning

- Check the area into which you will turn
- Warn your crew

Then

1 Move to the centre of the dinghy rotating tiller extension away from you without changing course

2 Extend the tiller arm

3 Push the tiller smoothly towards where you were sitting

4 Straighten the tiller as the sail begins to come across

5 Sit down and sail away

Whether the dinghy is centre or aft mainsheet rigged the process is the same

Notes

- At the start of the manoeuvre the dinghy should be flat.

- If you are gybing a centre main dinghy change hands when the gybe is complete. Face forward during the manoeuvre. Use the falls to initiate the gybe.

- If you are gybing an aft main dinghy change hands before you stand up. Face aft during the manoeuvre.

- In some dinghies the tiller extension may have to be rotated over the transom.

Notes

- During the learning period the instructor will instruct the crew, choose the appropriate time and place to turn and will be in full control of the dinghy. Once the process is mastered the instructor can pass control over to the student.

- The helmsman will then have to:

  Decide when it is appropriate to gybe.

  Check area into which he is going to turn.

  Warn the crew by calling out 'Stand by to gybe'

  As he pushes tiller extension firmly away call 'Gybe Oh!'

Train the crew to take the following action as the dinghy is turned

  When the helmsman calls 'Stand by to gybe' the crew uncleats jib sheet and checks area

  When he is ready, he answers 'Yes' to the call 'Stand by to gybe'

  Crew balances boat and sheets in jib

B Gybing - summary of the full manoeuvre

Gybing Aft Mainsheet	Gybing Centre Mainsheet
• Helmsman sits forward of the tiller and puts the boat on a training run • He checks inside the boat, particularly to see that the centreboard is only slightly down • He checks around the boat, especially the area into which he is going to sail and says 'Stand by to gybe' • Crew checks the area and says 'Yes' • Helmsman pulls in mainsheet to bring boom clear of shroud • He changes hands on mainsheet and tiller extension • He says 'Gybe oh' and moves towards middle of boat, taking tiller extension round and forward towards the other side • Demonstrate that, before the gybe, the extension swings right around the end of the tiller without the tiller itself being moved. • Helmsman initiates gybe by pushing the tiller extension towards where he was sitting and waits for the boom to swing across • As the mainsail clew lifts, the helmsman quickly centralises the tiller so that his weight, the boom and the tiller are simultaneously in the middle of the boat • Crew changes jib sheets and moves to centre of boat. • He sits out on the new windward side • Crew balances the boat and sets the jib once it has changed sides.	• The important difference about this drill is that the helmsman takes hold of the falls of the mainsheet to guide the boom across, preventing a violent gybe • Helmsman balances boat as necessary and checks all round - especially area into which boat is turning • He holds extension in dagger grip and calls 'Stand by to gybe' • Crew checks area and says 'Yes' • Helmsman steps back foot first into the middle of the boat whilst revolving extension over to new side without altering tiller itself • Helmsman holds falls of mainsheet • Crew moves into centre of boat and changes jib sheets. • Helmsman calls 'Gybe Oh', pushes tiller towards original sitting position and guides boom across with falls • As soon as boom starts to move, he centralises tiller and sits down on new windward side • Crew balances boat • Helmsman brings sheet hand back across in front of body to hold both tiller extension and sheet, thumb pointing towards end of tiller extension. He takes the mainsheet with his front hand and brings extension under arm to front of body • He trims mainsheet and settles down on new course • Crew trims jib sheet

A common fault in learning to gybe is to approach the manoeuvre too cautiously, often caused by the instructor. Children in Oppies will often gybe in preference to tacking, 'Because it's easier'. Build confidence and do smoothly inspiring demonstrations:

 • Gybe the boat at speed, leading to less pressure on the rig and a smoother turn

C Variations for Gybing

 • The variations in handling the tiller extension are the same as for tacking

 • With long tiller extensions, slide your hand down the extension before the gybe to reduce the angle through which you push the tiller

 • Holding the 'Falls' of the mainsheet to help the sail across only works with a 'true' centre main. Aft/Centre combinations can benefit from a pull on the sheet (e.g. Laser) but will not have the same effect

Session 11 Afloat
Gybing Practice

- Consider reefing

- Allow plenty of room (wind against tide if possible)

- Stay calm

- Stress that the mainsail should be as far out as possible (without touching the shroud). In missing this small but significant step students often have problems, especially in the medium and stronger breezes

- Facing straight across the boat when moving to the centre can avoid catching the mainsheet around the head, and encourages looking at the boom. 'Back foot forwards' then helps with turning to face forwards

Session 12 Afloat
Triangular course /First solo

- Triangular course: lay course with one leg to windward

- Sail with students and then move into the teaching boat

- Give instruction where necessary but avoid shouting from the teaching boat, bring students alongside if necessary

- Remember you are still responsible for the safety of boat and crew

Further sessions
In the course of the previous sessions students will have left and returned to base on several occasions. They can now go on to learn jetty work, man overboard, picking up moorings, coming alongside a moored boat etc with more intensity. You will be in and out of the dinghy, demonstrating particular skills and then watching progress from the shore or an escort boat. When setting courses for students, remember that you need to be able to communicate with them throughout using some of the skills explained in the single handers section.

Awareness of other boats will have been part of your teaching in the early stages. Stress it again now. Discuss 'Rule of the Road' problems as they occur and your solo crew will be less likely to become involved in collisions.

TOP TIP

Once you step out of the boat, things can go wrong for the student. Give them time to succeed.

Capsize Recovery Drill
Capsize recovery drill will fit into your programme at the earliest practical moment. Weather, water temperature and other considerations will influence your Senior Instructor's decision, but it is generally agreed that early capsizing is beneficial.

The end of a day's sailing provides the best opportunities for drying clothes, personal buoyancy and gear. Students are usually apprehensive about capsizing, and that apprehension can blunt the fine edge of their ability to learn. Once capsizing is over, they learn quickly and are less worried. You can also send them solo with a clearer conscience.

As an instructor, your responsibility is always to go into the water with your students during capsize drill. Right up to this stage, you have been teaching in close proximity to your students and it would seem strange if you now left them to fend for themselves. You cannot adequately control the drill from the escort boat, although it should, of course, be standing by. The drill must go smoothly and calmly to have the desired effect of building confidence.

- Always ensure that sufficient rescue cover is provided
- Shore briefing or drill using a dinghy tipped on its side
- Explain the scoop method
- Check personal and boat buoyancy
- Check students (contact lenses, glasses, watches and even false teeth!)
- Consider buoying the top of the mast if your boat inverts easily
- Your Senior Instructor is responsible for selecting a suitable site for the drill, away from hazards but close enough to base for safety and recovery
- You are responsible for tipping the boat over (wild swinging on the shrouds is unnecessary: a brisk tack with the mainsail sheeted well in and the crew staying on the old windward side of the boat should cause a gentle capsize)
- Smile, stay calm
- Direct operations from the bow of the boat so you can see both the person on the centreboard and the crew inside the boat
- Keep encouraging students but keep your physical assistance to a minimum
- The students will be much more confident if they have righted the dinghy without your help

TOP TIP

Consider free floating in deep water (buoy the mast head). Tethers and mooring ropes can make nervous students feel trapped

Repeat capsize until each student has succeeded but watch out for exhaustion or hypothermia problems after two or three attempts. It is better to stow the boat and gear after everyone has changed rather than risk difficulties with the cold, Maintain constant encouragement.

The six steps of the Scoop Method outlined in RYA book G3 for an aft mainsheet dinghy are repeated here in order to stress certain specific teaching points associated with each.

Step 1

- Both the crew swim to the stern. This reduces the risk of one becoming trapped if the boat inverts
- Helmsman checks that the rudder is secure and not floating off
- Crew finds the end of the mainsheet and gives it to the helmsman who, using it as a lifeline, swims around the outside of the boat to the centreboard and holds it or climbs onto it as necessary to prevent inversion
- Crew then swims along the inside of the boat to the centreboard case.

Following initial immersion, most students are still regaining their breath by the time the crew or helmsman has to go UNDER the mainsheet assembly to get clear round to the centreboard. Many try to swim over the top and some get their personal buoyancy hooked into the various floating bits of rope. Warn them of these difficulties.

Step 2

- The crew checks that the centreboard is fully down
- Helmsman holds onto it to prevent the boat inverting.

If the centreboard is not fully down, warn the crew of the risk of injury to the helmsman from an over-enthusiastic attempt to lower it without warning.

Step 3

- Crew finds the top (weather) jib sheet and throws it over to the helmsman, checks mainsheet is free

- Helmsman confirms that he has it

Confirmation of receipt is often inaudible, especially if the helmsman has failed to achieve it. The centreboard case is a useful slot through which to shout.

Step 4

Crew lies in the hull facing forwards and floats above the side-deck, holding on but taking care not to prevent the boat from righting.

Many students do not, initially, realise the great importance of this point. Some even disregard it, believing that they will be safer by hanging on.

Step 5

- Helmsman either lies back straight in the water with his feet on the boat's gunwale and hauls on the jib sheet

- Alternatively he climbs onto the centreboard, keeping his weight as close to the hull as possible to avoid breaking the board, and hauls on the jib sheet to right the dinghy with the crew member in it

TOP TIP

Face away from the boat and throw the jib sheet over your head - it's easier

Some find it difficult to get onto the centreboard. Any preliminary advice, which you can provide, is worth giving.
Heavyweights will be able to right the dinghy by the first method. With lightweights, the advice to keep as close to the hull as possible has to be modified in practice, as their weight is sometimes insufficient to provide the necessary righting moment. Stress the value of straight legs and back for maximum leverage.

Step 6

- With the jib backed the dinghy is hove-to and the crew is then able to help the helmsman aboard

- Helmsman may find that he can get into the boat as it comes upright

The right place for the helmsman to be brought aboard is beside the weather shroud. Discuss the option of rolling the boat to windward if you have a lightweight crew and a heavyweight helmsman.

In dinghies with open transoms, it may be more practical to re-enter over the stern. The problem with this method is that the boat tends to bear away around the person hanging on to the stern, so speed is necessary.

Further practical sessions

Man Overboard Recovery

Use dummy (fender and tyre), not a real person.

- Regain control immediately and turn onto a beam reach

- Maintain visual contact

- Sail away on beam to broad reach for 10 boat lengths, or enough to get the boat under control

- Tack and point the boat at the MOB

- Check the main will flap

- Bear away slightly if necessary so that final approach is on a close reach
- Spill and fill the mainsail to control boat speed
- Stop to leeward and immediately beside a MOB
- Helmsman goes forward and retrieves the MOB by the windward shroud
- A flick to windward on the tiller helps prevent the boat tacking on top of the MOB, who will act as a drogue or sea anchor to keep the dinghy in the basic hove-to position
- Repeat with helmsman as MOB, i.e. crew takes control of the boat

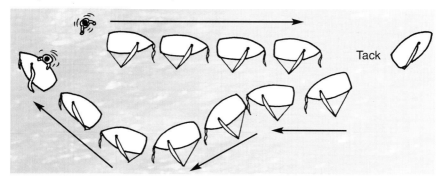

Tack

If it happened for real, the MOB should shout or whistle to gain attention but not swim about or he will rapidly lose body heat. If wearing personal buoyancy with additional oral inflation, he should inflate it, although it may need to be deflated for boarding.

Outline the aftercare needed for a real casualty.

Once your students have mastered the basic principles, encourage more realistic practice by briefing them that it should be the helmsman who 'falls overboard'. When the dummy is dropped over the side, the helmsman should let go of the tiller and mainsheet, move out of the way of the crew and take no further part in the manoeuvre. This results in the crew having to regain full control of the dinghy and achieves better results.

Coming alongside a moored boat or jetty/picking up a mooring

- Choose approach line and escape route
- Ensure sails will flap
- Drop mainsail if wind against or across tide
- Communication with crew

TOP TIP

Never force people to be competitive when introducing racing to another course. Allow them to find their own level of competitiveness.

Teaching racing - Level 2

Some Senior Instructors like to finish a Level 2 course by a practical assessment in which the students sail around a triangular course. Many centres complete the Level 2 course by organising a short informal race, thus encouraging students to consolidate their skills and introducing them to the competitive side of the sport. Assuming that you have covered the basic rules of the road, the minimum extra knowledge needed by students to complete this satisfactorily is an explanation of the typical port-hand triangular course and a basic starting procedure.

THE USE OF POWERED CRAFT IN A TEACHING OR COACHING ENVIRONMENT

Part of the skill of a dinghy instructor or coach is to be able to teach from a powerboat, which is why Powerboat Level 2 is necessary for dinghy instructors and club racing coaches.

Always wear the kill cord, attached securely to your leg or waist. If you fall overboard, how else will you ensure that the boat does not hit someone?

Don't shout from a moving powerboat to a moving dinghy unless the task demands it (eg coaching a fast moving boat). Instead, tell the students to stop and lie-to, before approaching the dinghy slowly from the windward side. Alternatively, overtake the dinghy to windward but on a parallel course. Cut the engine and offer advice as they sail past. Keep the prop away from people and ropes at all times.

A capsized boat should always be approached bow-to (techniques are given in G16 Safety Boat Handbook). Take care when approaching the shore to keep clear of people in the water and avoid damage to the prop.

The Level 2 course will include a knowledge of the basic equipment required. The sailing instructor should add to this as necessary.

See notes on coaching from a powerboat in the section on Advanced Instructor Training on page 88

TOP TIP

Always wear the kill cord

Always be aware of the propeller

For coaching or safety, positioning is everything

During an incident, count heads first

Stop the engine on arrival if there is someone in the water

TEACHING TECHNIQUES USING SINGLE HANDED DINGHIES

It is no accident that single handlers are so popular. Students are in control of their own boat right from the start. They are continuously at the helm and so cannot fail to benefit by practising new techniques and learning immediately from their mistakes. The boats themselves are simple, light and exciting to sail.

General points

Advantages

- Students continuously at the helm
- They learn faster
- Light
- Simple and exciting
- Particularly effective for teaching children
- Inexpensive to run
- Durable
- Low skill level required to succeed in some boats (Laser Funboat, Escape Mango)

Problems

- Can be frustrating at first
- Students tire easily
- Communication is harder
- Group control
- Cold quicker

You will be responsible for up to six students, possibly well scattered, at one time. Also, because students are always at the helm, possibly in lively boats, they will become tired more quickly.

Sessions should therefore be short and the instructor must always watch for signs of fatigue. Capsize is more likely in a single-handed than in the instructed larger dinghy, so suitable preparation must be made, as outlined below.

Environment

It is important to put your students in the right environment to achieve the tasks required.

Look at

- Equipment - the right size of boat and sail area for the size of student
- Wind strength
- Wind direction
- Temperature
- Sailing area
- Depth of water
- Starting point (beach/pontoon/bank/slipway)
- Length of sessions (short)

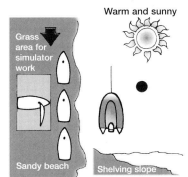

Warm and sunny

Grass area for simulator work

Sandy beach

Shelving slope

Group control

- Frequent briefings

- Recall signals (whistle and hand signals)

- Awareness of sailing area - diagrams, set course before students go afloat so they can see the boundaries

- Question students to check understanding

- Size of sailing area

- Use of 'buddy' system at first sessions

What if...?
Always consider

- What is the worst thing that could happen?

- What changes can you make to cope with this?

Communication

- Well thought out and structured briefings (include problems that might occur)

- Size of sailing area

- You should not have to shout to your students

- Students stop the boat and you go to them, or students come to you

- Be aware of the noise from an engine or a sail flapping

- If possible take a spare dinghy and sail with your students

- If students can see tasks they will pick them up quicker than simply being told

- Keep session short

- Good debrief

Capsize

Because your students are on their own and not very confident, you must point out:

- Righting a boat is easy

- It can be fun

- Wearing the right equipment means they will float in the water

- Demonstration from instructor first to show how easy it is

Even on a hot sunny day your students can get cold, once wet:

- Try to avoid capsize practice until the end of the day

- Try to keep them as dry as possible (consider reefing)

- Land drill where possible

Philosophy

The basic philosophy of the RYA Teaching Method outlined earlier applies just as much to single handed teaching as to conventional techniques, but at any stage you should ask yourself two questions:

- What do students already know and what is the minimum they need to know before they can complete the next session successfully?

This should save you unnecessary time ashore and save you teaching irrelevant details.

OUTLINE PROGRAMME FOR SINGLEHANDERS

The programme given below is just one of many which have been developed successfully. It is not intended to be definitive, merely to provide an introduction to the techniques needed.

Think of the timing of your shore sessions. You have to cover a lot before going afloat.

Session 1 Ashore
Clothing/footwear personal buoyancy/gear collection

- As for basic Method
- Consider dry suits and helmets
- Buoyancy aids are preferred to lifejackets

Session 2 Ashore
Rigging

- Reinforce wind direction
- Rig one boat first as a demonstration
- Students can rig their own boats
- Check each one before they go afloat

Session 3 Ashore
Tacking land drill/getting out of irons

- Demonstrate going about
- Reinforce wind direction
- Swing boat through the wind
- Demonstrate tacking using the method (centre main or aft mainsheet)
- Each student should then practise
- The instructor should then correct any faults
- Demonstrate getting out of irons (push/push, pull/pull)

Session 4 Afloat
Practise tacking/Beam reach/Starting and stopping

- Boats rigged
- Demonstrate launching one boat
- Instructor demonstrates what is to be done. Remember, actions are more effective than words
- Instructor in the water
- Check student's orientation is correct
- Before letting go, go through sailing position, starting and stopping, tacking (walk boat through tack)
- Once ready send off on way to buoy
- Talk student through tack
- Talk student back to you, stopping the boat by you
- Once each student has had a go, set up a beam reach figure of eight course

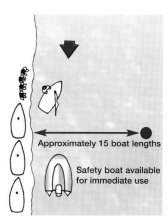

Approximately 15 boat lengths

Safety boat available for immediate use

Session 5 Ashore and afloat
Turning towards and away from the wind

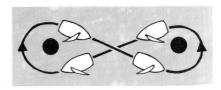

- Lay course as shown

- Move buoy further into wind as session continues

- Brief clearly using board or diagram

- Demonstrate ashore or afloat the sail positions as boat turns towards and away from the wind

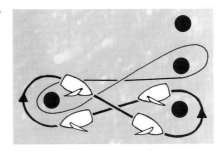

- Reinforce wind direction at each step

- Use four steps for getting from beam reach to close hauled

- Students practise

- Go afloat one boat at a time to revise session 4

- Move buoy up in stages

- Debrief ashore at end of session

Session 6 Ashore and afloat
Going to windward

- Lay course as shown

- Brief clearly using board or diagram

- Reinforce no-go-zone

- Demonstrate in water or on simulator, effects on sail

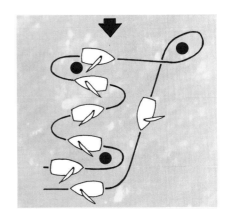

- Revise luffing up and bearing away

- Demonstrate

- Send off students one at a time at intervals

- Introduce the Five Essentials to this exercise

Session 7 Ashore and afloat
Gybing practice

- Demonstrate on land using the method (centre main/aft main)

- Training run

- Dagger board position

- Reinforce Five Essentials

- Allow each student to practise

Session 8 Afloat
Triangular Course

- Lay course as shown
- Demonstrate to students
- Send students off one at a time at intervals
- Move mark B until AB and BC become training runs
- Avoid dead runs and death rolls caused by sailing by the lee
- Debrief ashore

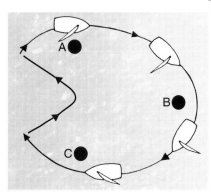

General comments

- Keep sessions short and intensive
- Clear briefings are essential
- Debrief each session
- Lay marks between sessions so your students can see the course before setting off
- Check equipment before the course begins

In ideal conditions, with above average students and good support, Sessions 1 to 8 can be completed in a single long day. It is far more practical, however, to treat this as two days of instruction, which is the usual time taken for an RYA Level 1 course.

Single handers are particularly appropriate for teaching children.

Further sessions
Coming alongside

- Same principles apply
- Can only be achieved in wind against tide conditions by releasing the mainsail completely or releasing the clew

Lee shore landings

- Explain when to raise dagger board and rudder and when to ease kicker
- Release clew as soon as possible before recovery

Manoeuvres such as collecting objects in the water, using the MOB technique and sailing up to moorings are good boat handling practice.

If your students are working towards their Level 2 certificate, you now have several days to consolidate the basic techniques and cover the onshore teaching and jetty work etc afloat.

You will already have used a number of buoys to establish short courses for the early sessions. Introduce students to the slalom course, which is an ideal compact way of encouraging tacking and gybing practise. Guidance on how to make up and lay a slalom is given in the section on mark laying (page 74).

The following are games to reinforce sailing skills taken from the NSSA publication *Sailing Across the Curriculum.*

Duck Hunt Catch

With the group afloat or awaiting a Le Mans start on the whistle, the 'ducks' are spread over the sailing area. The winner is the person or team to collect the greatest number.

Variation: Award points by 'duck' colour, size or marking. The winner is still the one with the highest score but this offers a more tactical game.

Teaching points: Going about, gybing, awareness of other boats, avoiding collisions.

Resources: Plastic containers/half inflated balloons containing a little water to stop them blowing away.

Orienteering afloat

As for land orienteering by using buoys marked with code letters.

A GAME OF TAG IS GOOD FOR HONING SKILLS

Teaching points: sailing on all points of the wind.

Resources: Buoys coloured or marked with code letters.

Tag

One boat is 'it', raises dagger board half way, throws tennis ball at other boats. If it hits, then struck boat is 'it', retrieves tennis ball, raises dagger board half-way and chases other boats. Useful to play when using different types of boats - Oppies and Toppers.

Teaching points: Use of centre/dagger board, speed control.

Resources: Tennis ball, large buoyant sponge, buoyant Frisbee.

Relays

Team event to transport baton/piece of equipment/person from one shore to another.

Variations: transport to a boat, race round a slalom course, collect gear required for a task. All of these need very clear instructions about changeover procedures, what and how objects can be carried, time penalties etc.

Teaching points: sailing accurately on all points of sailing, landing on lee shore, leaving lee shore.

Resources:

Buckets, tennis balls, corks

Rounders

This is not a team game, each boat tries to beat the scores of all the other boats. In turn, all boats come alongside the anchored rescue boat - the base. The 'batting' boat throws a ball in any direction and then sails around the buoys. Each buoy rounded scores a rounder. Fielding boats retrieve balls and either hit the batting boat or return the ball to base.

Teaching points: reaching, coming alongside

Resources: one tennis ball, 4 to 6 boats

Topper race all standing

Race around a triangular course without sitting down in the boat (tack by walking around the mast or by stepping between boom and sail foot; gybe by stepping around sail clew).

Teaching points: Boat balance and trim

Resources: Three buoys

Treasure Hunt

Mix clues both onshore and on-the-water. Have each team follow a completely different order of clues. End with a picnic or barbecue when the 'treasure' is discovered. (Have some treasure for everyone, not just the first team). Add to the fun with pirate costumes!

Teaching points: Accurate and fast sailing, team building.

Resources: Laminated clue sheets, face paints, box of dressing up clothes, 'treasure'.

More advanced techniques

The majority of teaching in single-handers is aimed at beginners, covering Levels 1 and 2 of the RYA National Sailing Scheme. Much of the content of Seamanship Skills courses - concerned with traditional boat handling skills - is inappropriate to single-handers but the same cannot be said for racing techniques.

Single-handers are popular for teaching many aspects of the Start Racing course, as their simplicity of handling allows helmsmen to concentrate on learning and practising the skills of strategy and tactics. Many of the exercises used are concerned with improving boat handling techniques and as such are valuable to all students who have mastered the basic skills of sailing.

Conclusion

Try to maintain an atmosphere of controlled excitement during training. The boats are exciting in themselves but it is up to you to keep the students occupied and learning all the time.

Remember that the programme above is just one of many which have been developed successfully over the years. Another aimed specifically at younger children is outlined in the Club Guide. Although children may be more adept at developing new skills, their attention span may be much shorter and so the same techniques are covered over a longer period, interspersed with other activities.

There is no single 'right' way; each club or centre will develop its own programme best suited to its needs. All, however, will follow the same broad philosophy of training.

MARK LAYING FOR SHORT COURSES

When running single-handed, improvers or racing sessions, you will need to lay a succession of short, easily moved courses. To avoid problems, remember the following points:

- Keep marks as simple as possible

- Avoid complicated systems with blocks and weights; Sinkers are cheaper and less trouble than anchors

- Always lay marks over the windward side of your teaching boat.Have the warp flaked ready, with the sinker on top ready to go. Retrieve marks in the same way

- Reflake neatly as you haul in

- Lay a warp only just longer than the depth of water

- Don't use warps which float (polypropylene)

- A range of marks of different colours makes identification easier

- Carry a burgee or wind indicator as an aid to laying accurate courses relative to the wind

- Carry a compass to aid laying precise course angles

- It is sometimes easier to lay a mark in approximately the right place, and then tow it into its exact position. Sinkers make this easier than anchors

- Have a simple communication system if working with a mother ship or committee boat

- Don't be afraid to move a course after large wind shifts

Slalom courses

Simple slalom courses can be used by almost every group of students for concentrated practice. The most rudimentary system is simply a number of buoys, laid individually, each with their own sinker.

Laying this requires considerable work, especially in deep water, and means even more work after large wind shifts. It is far better to make up a linked system using a long ground line and a number of risers, each one with a buoy.

In non-tidal waters each ground line needs only one anchor, laid at the windward end of the slalom, but in wind against tide or wind across tide conditions, the ground line will have to be anchored at each end. The length of each riser need only be slightly greater than the maximum draught of your fleet (including the teaching boat), with a small weight at the bottom to keep the riser vertical and the ground line low. A quick release system for attaching risers to the ground line makes it easier to modify the slalom - altering the distance between buoys according to weather conditions, students' abilities and the type of training The most common arrangement for slalom buoys is shown in the diagram. It can be used as a 'funnel' for repeated tacking, with the wing mark set to keep boats clear of the slalom when heading back to the start.

Exactly the same layout serves for downwind practice, but the intention here is that students should gybe around each buoy in turn. It is conventional to put the wing mark on the starboard side of the course this time, in order that students will be approaching the top of the slalom on starboard tack.

To lay this course you will need two of the downwind strings of buoys described above, together with the isolated wing mark. It takes a certain finesse to get the mark spacing correct relative to the students' abilities.

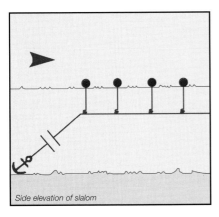

Side elevation of slalom

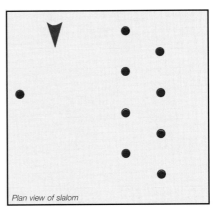

Plan view of slalom

It is impossible to be dogmatic about how many boat lengths' separation are needed for different abilities - it's probably better to define the spacing as enough to allow the student to recover from the manoeuvre of rounding one buoy, settle down and plan the next rounding before he has to do it. Anything less than about four boat lengths is going to be counter-productive even for the most experienced sailor, as the boat will have to be thrown into the manoeuvres without any planning or style.

If the double string is too complicated, you can still achieve a great deal with a single slalom line. All it takes is a little more self-discipline by the student to ensure that he does tack or gybe at each buoy as appropriate.

By alternating the colours of the buoys in each string, you can build in different levels of ability; stage one is simply to use all the buoys of one colour; stage two is to use all the buoys.

The final development is to lay a slalom consisting of a double string narrowing down to a single string, with the spacing getting progressively narrower.

TEACHING THE ADVANCED MODULES IN THE NATIONAL SAILING SCHEME

TEACHING SEAMANSHIP SKILLS

Manoeuvres

Many of these are a revision and refinement of skills learnt on a Level 2 course. Nevertheless, during a 2-day course you may only have time to teach the skills required without a great deal of further coaching. Each technique can be broken down into four stages:

- Planning

- Approach

- Manoeuvre

- Escape

A briefing and demonstration or land drill ashore can be used for many techniques.

Practice doesn't necessarily make perfect - it may serve only to repeat poor technique and hence reinforce mistakes. That's where you come in.

Provide goals for their performance by setting precise areas in which to anchor and make the target progressively smaller.

Give an incentive for a good reef by requiring the students to sail to windward after taking it in. Provide goals for good lee shore landings or alongside practice by having prizes on the beach or jetty.

Ideally, bring all the manoeuvres together once they have been learnt into the framework of a seamanship exercise or, if you want to make it competitive, a seamanship game.

The principle is just that you combine the exercises in a way which will make their practice more enjoyable and their execution more efficient. The golden rule about such games is to keep them simple. As soon as you get bogged down in penalty points and the like, the fun will evaporate.

If, on the other hand, the game is packaged properly, your students won't have time to realise that you are simply providing structured practice. It could be marketed as an obstacle course or treasure hunt full of local interest.

Working from a teaching boat

With many of the topics outlined above, the instructor may first be in the sailing dinghy, but then is most likely to be out of it, allowing the students to practise under supervision. As soon as you get out of the dinghy your communication problems increase. Read the section on Coaching on page 88.

Reefing afloat

- When to reef - purpose

- Where to reef - away from hazards, starboard tack if possible

- How - order of events, co-ordination between helm and crew

- How much - appearance of reefed sail, i.e. efficient shape, boom not drooped, no wrinkles, kicking strap still effective

- Genoa changed to jib and centreboard raised slightly if necessary

Anchoring

Briefing ashore

- Type of anchor and selection of suitable anchorage

- Nature of bottom

- Shelter

- Depth (changes with tide)

- Length of warp

Afloat

- Approach on close reach or against tidal stream

- Drop main if wind against tide

- Lower anchor when boat stops

- Pay out warp

- Check holding with transits

- Stow sails.

Being Towed By A Powerboat

- Good communication

- Approach

- Pass tow line

- Drop mainsail

- Secure towline

- Bridle/strong points

- Quick release system

- Being towed alongside

- Springs

- Being towed stern first

- Centreboard up

- Crew weight aft

- Steer if possible.

Sailing without a rudder, or with an elastic loop over the tiller

- Raise centreboard to 3/4 down
- Rudder can be raised rather than removed, alternatively elastic loop is thick but loose allowing some tiller movement
- Jib in, main out to bear away
- Main in to luff up
- Boats usually have slight weather helm when both sails filling
- If rudder raised keep weight forward
- Heel to windward to bear away
- Heel to leeward to luff up
- Slow movements across the boat
- Can be easier if jib sheets tied together and mainsheet reeved as a simple purchase
- Following gybe keep jib to windward until settled on new course to prevent spinning

Sailing without a centreboard

- Explain the underwater shape of the dinghy
- Discuss lateral resistance and how this can be increased by moving the crew weight forward

Sailing Backwards

- Explain the context, which is usually escaping from a crowded mooring
- Centreboard at least half down
- Explain the need to bring the dinghy head to wind
- Push the boom so that the sail backs
- Explain the importance of steering by looking backwards (the dinghy follows the direction that the rudder is pointing)

Road Trailers and Towing

- Discuss security of dinghy on road trailer
- Discuss towing regulations (lighting, speed restrictions, number plate visibility etc.)

TEACHING DAY SAILING SKILLS

Navigation

- Dinghy navigation is really pilotage
- You cannot do detailed chart work in a dinghy
- Pre-planning is essential

Charts

- Chart datum
- Measuring distances from latitude scale
- Soundings
- Drying heights
- Heights above mean high water springs
- Conspicuous features, lighthouses, headlands etc
- Common hazards, rocks, wrecks, overfalls etc

Compass

- Compass rose
- Variation - corrections
- Awareness of deviation

Tide tables

- High and low water
- Correction for BST
- Springs and neaps
- Rule of twelfths/percentage rule

Food and drink

- Suitable clothing
- Harbour regulations
- Avoiding shipping
- Where to moor or beach at destination

Planning and Pilotage

- Sailing a passage, which has first been planned
- Consideration of tide and weather conditions, traffic etc.
- Use laminated charts and chinagraph pencil

Pilotage is usually a visual exercise rather than sailing for long distances on a compass bearing. If you know where you are, with a chart and compass you should be able to identify where to go next.

- Courses and distances on chart
- Sail on transits to avoid being set sideways by tide
- At known positions eg buoys, confirm position or alter course

Emergencies

- Pin point red flares

- Orange smoke flares

- Combined day/night flares are also a possibility

Meteorology

Sources of weather information

- Television/Radio - shipping forecast, local forecast (details in nautical almanac)

- Weather fax/text forecasts by mobile phone/telephone

- Internet and email forecasts

- Newspapers

- Coastguard

- Harbour master

Terms used in shipping forecasts

- Beaufort scale

- Backing and veering

- Good, moderate and poor visibility

Weather patterns

- Rapid barometric change usually indicates strong winds

- Anticlockwise wind circulation around lows

- Clockwise wind circulation around highs

- Warm front - lowering cloud, decreasing visibility, drizzle, south west winds

- Cold front - veer, cooler, north west wind, clear, showery

- Sea breeze - air over warm land rises, cool sea, air drawn ashore

- Fog - advection: warm air over cool sea, or radiation: land cools

Observation afloat

- Squalls

- Gusts

- Approach of low pressure - cirrus clouds, hazy sun

Decision Making

- Planning for difficult conditions

- Alternative destinations

- The effect of wind and tide on sea conditions

TEACHING SAILING WITH SPINNAKERS
Spinnaker hoists

There are a number of ways to hoist the spinnaker, depending on the situation.

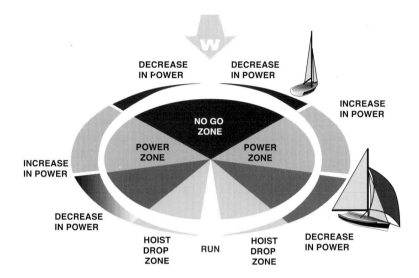

Conventional spinnaker - Leeward hoist (or spinnaker chute hoist)

- Crew puts pole on
- Helm hoists spinnaker and balances boat
- Crew takes the guy and cleats, then sits on windward side deck
- Helm sits to leeward
- Crew takes sheet and adjusts as necessary

Conventional spinnaker - Windward hoist

- Crew gathers spinnaker up into a ball and checks that the spinnaker guy is free
- Crew throws the spinnaker forward and the helm hoists quickly
- Communication is very important, otherwise the spinnaker will end up under the bow of the boat
- Crew puts pole on whilst helm plays the guy and the sheet
- Crew takes the guy and sits to windward
- Helm sits to leeward
- Crew takes the sheet and adjusts as necessary

Asymmetric spinnaker - hoist

- Helm bears away until the boat is in the hoist/drop zone, i.e. broad reach
- Crew pulls pole out

- Helm adjusts pole alignment if necessary (RS400 etc]
- Crew hoists spinnaker
- Helm luffs as crew sheets in
- As the boat accelerates the helm bears away and the crew eases the sheet
- Communication paramount to keep the boat achieving maximum VMG (velocity made good) i.e. sailing as low as possible but not losing the increased apparent wind strength, which enables the boat to sail low.

Spinnaker gybing

Again, there are a number of ways to share jobs during the gybe

Conventional

- As the helm bears away the crew releases the guy and pivots the spinnaker around to windward
- Helm gybes the mainsail
- Crew stands up and swaps the pole to the new side whilst the helm balances the boat and plays both the guy and sheet
- Crew takes over the guy and sits on new windward side, helm sits to leeward
- Crew takes sheet and adjusts as necessary
- On a run to run gybe, helm may control the spinnaker and the crew gybe the main with the kicker

Asymmetric

- Choose a good place to gybe when the boat is travelling fast
  (down the face of a wave) and in clear water
- Helm may centralise pole
- Helm bears away and gybes the main, steering carefully throughout the manoeuvre
- Whilst the helm is bearing away the crew gradually eases the sheet to assist the spinnaker to slide through the slot in front of the jib, then releases the old sheet and pulls quickly on the new sheet
- Helm re-aligns the pole (RS400 etc)
- Helm will probably have to luff slightly to pick up the apparent wind and then bear away as the boat speed increases.
- Crew eases sheet as boat bears away

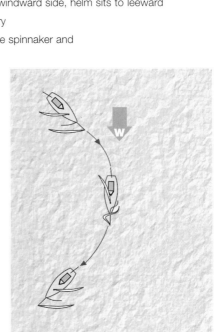

Hoist Zone

Spinnaker drop

Bag

- Crew hands sheet to helm to play whilst pole is being removed
- Crew takes the pole off the mast and then off the spinnaker clew and then stores it
- Helm releases spinnaker halyard and crew pulls the spinnaker down on the windward side, working up the leech first and then along the foot (this reduces the chance of the spinnaker twisting on the next hoist)
- Meanwhile the helm is looking ahead ready for the mark rounding

Asymmetric

- Crew either hands sheet to helm to play or stands on it (this enables the spinnaker to be kept flying for longer, keeps the boat moving faster and keeps the spinnaker out of the water during the drop)
- Crew pulls in excess retrieval line (to stop spinnaker going under the bow and to speed up the drop)
- Crew uncleats pole outhaul and halyard and pulls spinnaker down by retrieval line
- As this is happening, the helm releases the pole alignment controls (if applicable), balances the boat and looks ahead ready for the mark rounding.

Design and Performance

Fat deep hull shapes tend to be slow (Wayfarer, Enterprise), though boats with a lot of rocker tend to sail fast and cleanly in waves, and be easier to launch through waves (Scorpion). Skiff type hull shapes would basically skim rather than plough and need to be light in weight to assist planing (29er, RS800). Once planing, they sail fast downwind, requiring accurate and smooth helming. Sailing fast downwind reduces pressure on the rig, so they can be easier to gybe.

Sails with full length battens (RS400) produce a lot of power but can be hard to read and do not de-power easily, so it can be difficult to stop the boat or control it ashore. Boats with a conventional spinnaker can sail directly downwind. In contrast, those with asymmetric spinnakers zigzag downwind, sailing at higher speeds but travelling further. Intermediate skiff designs (RS400, Laser 4000) often have spinnaker poles which 'cant' to windward, enabling them to sail deeper downwind than would be possible with a fixed pole.

THE INSTRUCTOR COURSE MODERATION/ASSESSMENT

Following the five days of your Instructor training, your course will be moderated by an RYA Coach/Assessor to confirm whether you match up to the qualities of an RYA Instructor outlined at the beginning of this handbook. The purpose of the moderation is also to ensure that RYA Instructor courses are run to the correct standards as specified by the RYA.

The moderation will usually take place immediately after the training course, but there are some advantages in delaying it until you have had time to put all the theory of instructional technique into practice. If your training Coach feels that you are not yet ready for assessment immediately after training, he will probably recommend that you wait until you have brushed up on some of your techniques or gained more confidence from assisting qualified instructors.

Before the moderation starts, the Assessor will agree with you a plan for the day, so that you can show evidence of your competence in instructional ability afloat and ashore. The specific items involved are: practical instruction afloat, a prepared teaching activity, shore drills and written paper, although for convenience the paper may have been given during the training course.

If you feel slightly apprehensive about the moderation, try to think of the Assessor as both a detective and a judge. You stand accused of being a competent instructor - the Assessor's job is to gather enough evidence to get a conviction! In other words, you should be working together to ensure that your ability exceeds the minimum standard set, so that in turn students on RYA courses can be sure of receiving accurate instruction in a safe, enjoyable environment.

Practical instruction based on RYA teaching methods

Whenever possible, this will be done with beginners. The usual arrangement is for a group of people to be brought in specifically for you to teach, and it is very important that they are properly briefed on their role.

It is also likely that the Assessor will have to play the part of a beginner or an improver at some stage in the assessment, so that he can test your teaching over a range of skills properly. When this happens, he will explain the role he is going to play and the ability, which he has. If you are in any doubt about his briefing, please ask him to explain further.

The Assessor will be looking for

- The ability to plan the session according to the needs of your students

- A friendly, supportive manner towards your students, from their arrival to departure

- The boat rigged according to weather conditions and the abilities of your students

- Adequate boat control at all times

- Teaching according to the methods outlined on your course and in this book, progressing according to the students' abilities

- Correct positioning of instructor and students

- Successful demonstrations and clear explanations

- Correct diagnosis and tactful correction of students' faults.

- Use of lying-to position for crew changes and briefings

It is far more natural for you to be teaching beginners than for another instructor or the Assessor to play the role of a student, but if the latter is necessary the Assessor will take account of the false situation.

When beginners are used, the Assessor will also be assessing you through their reaction, looking for the three key factors, which are important for successful teaching:

- Are the students safe?

- Are they learning anything valuable?

- Are they enjoying themselves?

No particular weighting is put on any one of these three, as they are inter-related. The good instructor is the one who meets each of these goals all the time.

Prepared 10 minute talk/training activity

The Assessor will not expect you to be a professional lecturer or a polished orator; in fact the title of this part of the assessment is deliberately chosen to allow a practical bias. He will be looking for the following:

- Overall format clear - introduction, development and summary

- Audible, interesting voice - right speed of presentation

- Accurate, relevant content - sufficient material but not way beyond the demands of the syllabus

- Essential points emphasised and summarised

- Teaching aids prepared and used as appropriate

- Difficulties discovered and explained

- Questions prompted and answered

The most common faults of nervous, inexperienced instructors are to try to cram too much detail into the time available and then rush through it by speaking too quickly. During your preparation, remember to split the content up into:

- What must be covered

- What should be covered

- What could be covered

Then rehearse to see how it fits into the time available. You can then edit the talk by cutting out or shortening some of the less important detail.

Practical demonstration of shore drills

The assessor may expect you to cover tiller extension drills for aft and/or centre mainsheet dinghies. Before doing so, he will have discussed with your training Coach the techniques used during the course, in case there are any local differences from the drills outlined in this handbook.

The Assessor is not trying to catch you out by minute attention to detail, but he will be looking for:

- A brief explanation of why drills are used
- Adequate preparation (and explanation) of equipment
- Good positioning of students
- Clear accurate demonstrations, both at normal speed and slowly with commentary
- Ability to identify and correct students' faults

The written paper

Although the written paper forms part of your assessment as an RYA Instructor, it is included under the 'training' part of the course as a practical necessity. It is difficult enough for the visiting Assessor to conduct all the practical parts of the assessment in one day, let alone invigilate and mark a written paper.

Conventionally, it will be scheduled into the programme towards the end of the course, and it is designed with two objectives in mind. The first is to confirm that there are no large gaps in the background knowledge of the subjects you are intending to teach; the second is to provide an assessment of those areas of teaching, which cannot realistically be covered by practical assessment.

Literary or artistic excellence is not required, but you will have to prove that you understand both the facts and how best to put them across. The paper should not be seen as a test of literacy and may be completed in other ways.

Overall assessment

It is usual for a number of candidates to be assessed on the same day and this will result in some time when you are not directly under the attention of the Assessor, but he may still be keeping a distant eye on your work.

Throughout the moderation, in addition to considering the detailed points outlined above, the Assessor will be making an overall (or holistic) judgement, based on the criteria and measured against his experience of the sport. The qualities sought can be summarised as:

- Enthusiasm for the sport
- Confidence in the subject
- Teaching ability
- Awareness
- Anticipation

At some point, often at the middle of the day, he will seek comments from the training Coach, who has been monitoring your progress throughout the course and so has a good idea of your ability. This will help the Assessor to take account of any particular circumstances on the day.

The Assessor and training coach will review your performance with you. This debrief may include several more questions, to ensure that you have sufficient understanding of different aspects of work as an instructor.

Finally, the training Coach and Assessor will confirm whether or not you have yet proved your competence as an RYA Dinghy Instructor, complete the necessary paperwork and agree an action plan with you for the future. Such a plan will help you to overcome any gaps in your knowledge or ability, if for some reason you are not entirely successful in the assessment.

If you disagree with the decision, he will discuss the way in which someone else can re-assess you, or the procedure for appeal to the RYA.

ADVANCED INSTRUCTOR TRAINING

The Advanced Instructor must have the background knowledge, technical ability and skills to demonstrate any of the Sailing with Spinnakers and Performance Sailing courses. Teaching people how to sail performance dinghies requires a subtle change in the attitude of the Instructor. There are many different skills to learn from a coaching point of view. While many people will wish to receive coaching or instruction in race standard Wayfarers or GP14s, many of the newer boats will be a lot faster, so adapt your coaching style to suit. While your students will know the basic skills required to get the boat from A to B, you have to be able to analyse their performance, give positive feedback and coach them progressively. It goes without saying that you must be confident in sailing the dinghies in which you are coaching.

Boat Set Up
This will include general principles and use of rig controls

Boat Handling
Including use of symmetric and asymmetric spinnakers, trapezing and safety

Coaching
Candidates will be encouraged to develop a positive but relaxed style, which brings about improvement in those being coached

Use of the Powerboat
Safe and effective driving and positioning for coaching and safety

Advanced Instructor candidates are referred to the relevant chapters of the Advanced Handbook G12 for more information

There are a number of areas where the Advanced Instructor will focus.

Briefing.
The briefing is vitally important because high performance dinghies could be spread out over a far larger area than a fleet of Toppers. Make certain of your briefing:

- Clear and concise (use pictures and diagrams)

- Safety and recall signals understood by everyone

- The session aims are clear

- The learning objectives are clear and understood by all students. This is especially important in a group of mixed ability

- The sailing area is suitable for the purpose of the session. Downwind sailing in a breeze will require much more space than roll tacking practice in light winds

- Use bullet points and don't waffle

- Use effective questioning to make sure everyone understands what is going to happen on the water

- Don't try and cover too much in each session - concentrate on "bite size chunks"

Land Drills
Due to the nature of the dinghies and the subject matter involved, the use of land drills is highly recommended. See the notes on land drills on page 26

Exercises which can benefit from land drills include:

- Spinnaker hoists, gybes and drops
- Trapeze work
- Sail setting and sail controls. This is also an excellent way to make sure that all dinghies are set up correctly for the conditions
- Tacking and gybing practice

Demonstrate and then give the students time to practice, using positive coaching all the time. Take care that no one will get hurt falling off a trapeze or falling out of a dinghy whilst dropping a spinnaker etc

Demonstrations

The use of demonstrations is a valuable tool in the Advanced Instructor's armoury. This is why it is of paramount importance that you as the Instructor can competently sail performance dinghies. Areas of coaching that benefit from demonstrations include:

- Tacking and gybing
- Mark rounding
- Spinnaker hoist, gybe and drop

Coaching

Effective coaching whilst on the water is one of the most important aspects of becoming an Advanced Instructor. The ability to assess the performance of a dinghy or student and make a valid contribution to their improvement is fundamental to your role.

TOP TIP

Try not to shout, particularly upwind

- Be effective. If you don't have anything useful to say, don't say anything!
- Be positive. Sailing is fun
- Keep it short and simple (KISS). Don't overload your students
- Try and reduce stress levels, people perform much better if they are relaxed
- Be precise and don't waffle. Tell them exactly how to improve. For clarity use the same words as you used when briefing where possible
- Don't try and shout across an expanse of water, get them to stop and come alongside – it saves time in the long run
- Make notes whilst on the water to assist your debrief

Use of the Powerboat

The best strategy is usually to float free or anchor, calling boats over for input. However you may wish to observe and coach boats sailing at high speeds. Constant vigilance is essential. The ability to drive a powerboat well and control its position in relation to a fast moving dinghy is a skill that only comes with practice. Whilst on the water, even though you may have half a dozen boats in your group, you will often be working in a one to one scenario and then moving on to the next boat whilst the others practice.

Specific points regarding coaching from a moving powerboat:

- ALWAYS have the kill cord attached to you. A RIB travelling at speed with no driver is extremely dangerous
- Can they hear you? Get close and give clear and concise instructions

- Safety – downwind position your powerboat just to windward and level with the dinghy's transom. If someone falls overboard, will you avoid them? If going upwind you may be just to leeward, so you are clear if the boat tacks

- Most performance dinghies are not easy boats to stop and lie-to, so draw clear diagrams or instructions on a white board for the students to see as they sail past.

- If alongside a boat with racks or wings rest the wing on the side of the powerboat. This is sometimes called the "secure lie-to"

- Types of powerboat – most performance boats are fairly fragile so RIBs with console steering are the best choice.

- Positioning yourself relative to the group. Depending on the session you will need to position your coach boat in the correct place to enable effective coaching. These are:

1 Tacking exercise; coach boat to leeward of the fleet

2 Gybing exercise; coach boat to windward of the fleet

3 Windward mark rounding; coach boat to windward of the mark

4 Leeward mark rounding; coach boat to windward of the mark or use coach boat as the leeward mark

5 Trapezing, spinnaker work or boat speed exercise; follow individual dinghies

6 Starting practice; coach boat at windward end of the line and on the line

- If using a camera, it is strongly recommended that someone else drives the boat

TOP TIPS

Asymmetric Coaching and Instructing

When hoisting the asymmetric the helm should bear away to the hoist/drop zone and then keep the boat flat by steering rather than by moving their weight around.

Before gybing in strong winds, get the boat moving as fast as possible and well balanced, steer quickly and smoothly through the gybe, keeping the boat flat at all times.

When dropping the asymmetric apply the same techniques as hoisting, i.e. during the drop keep the boat flat by steering rather than moving crew weight.

Try to anticipate gusts; as a gust hits, bear away and sail lower without easing the sails much. The apparent wind will move forward as your speed increases therefore the boat's angle to the apparent wind will remain roughly constant.

If racing in dinghies with fully battened mains, keep the kicker eased slightly during pre-start manoeuvres. This will stop the boat becoming stuck in-irons at the critical moment.

When roll tacking and gybing in light winds, be careful not to catch the wings or racks in the water by rolling too far. This would slow the boat considerably.

A lot of asymmetric dinghies are very skiff-shaped with little rocker. In light winds trim the bow down to keep the transom clear of the water. Quite often the crew sits in front of the mast and completes tacks and gybes from there.

Debrief

The debrief is very important. You must give positive feedback from the session on the water. Very often your debrief will be analytical and will deal with a number of small but specific points. It may involve going back to a land drill to demonstrate a point or specific manoeuvre. Always try and involve all of the students and find a positive point for them all.

Debrief points to remember:

- Use the Traffic Light for feedback (see page 24)
- Be specific
- Analyse each dinghy's performance individually
- Relate performance to session aims as well as what actually happened on the water
- Involve all of the students
- Be positive, (a lot of students will be ecstatic at just having sailed an RS200 with a kite up, so don't pull their performance to pieces!)
- Don't be afraid to go back to a land drill – it will reinforce their learning
- Remember it's fun, they should want to go back on the water to improve their sailing

TOP TIP

When gybing, ensure your students look where they are going and make small adjustments to the helm all the way through - 'Steer through the gybe'.

Safety.

Sailing high performance dinghies always involves capsizing at some point. The ability to capsize, right the dinghy and sail on is an essential skill when racing high performance boats. It is important that you make your students aware of the particular risks, which can be involved. Useful issues can include:

- Clothing. Make sure all students have the correct personal equipment required for sailing a performance dinghy. Wetsuits or dry suits, good quality gloves, trapeze harness that fits correctly, dinghy or wetsuit boots, buoyancy aid that is suitable (i.e. high fit that gives plenty of room for movement)
- Knife. Advise that they should all carry a knife that can be used to cut themselves clear of the boat or equipment
- Run a positive safety session before your students go afloat. Don't put your students off, but make them aware of relevant issues on the day:

  1 The lack of an air pocket under many high performance dinghies when inverted

  2 The risk of being caught on rigging with a trapeze harness

  3 The risk of injury during a high-speed wipe-out
- Make sure that all dinghies being used are safe. Tape up any sharp areas or fittings, make sure that wire is not fraying, check all fittings and control lines on a regular basis.
- Ascertain the ability of all students before going afloat. You can always increase the challenge, but lost confidence is difficult to replace.

RACING INSTRUCTOR TRAINING

During instructor training, coaches may sign up those candidates who demonstrate sufficient competence as racing instructors. The minimum experience required is that candidates have completed a minimum of eight club races and have assisted the club race officer. The decision to sign off the endorsement is at the discretion of the coaching team.

Introduction

The majority of dinghy sailing in Britain takes place in clubs; most clubs organise dinghy racing which is a main focus of their activities. Many people learn to sail each year but can be put off the sport when faced for the first time with the apparent complexities of club racing.

The Racing Instructor course is designed to enable Dinghy Instructors to introduce relatively inexperienced sailors to club racing. All RYA Instructor courses should include approximately half a day of practical training on the subject.

It may also be run as a stand alone course of minimum duration one day.

The course should include the following characteristics:

• An emphasis on racing as fun

• Ensuring that starts and rules are not intimidating

• The provision of enough information for Level 2 standard sailors to get round a club racing course safely, without presenting a hazard to other sailors

• Encouragement to sailors to start racing, join a club and progress within the sport

The Course and Starting Sequence

Club Course

Most clubs will have fixed buoys with a system to identify them. The course used will depend upon the wind direction on the day. It will normally be posted as a list of buoys in the order they are to be rounded and which side to leave them on (port or starboard) e.g. SL (Start Line) Ep Bs Dp Ap SL 3 laps

Trapezoid with outer loop

Popular open meeting course, especially with youth classes. These types of course are also extremely good when sailing multiple classes on the same course - different loops can be specified for different classes. This keeps the classes apart on the water.

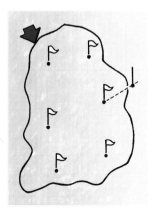

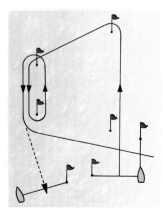

Trapezoid with inner loop

Popular open meeting course, as above.

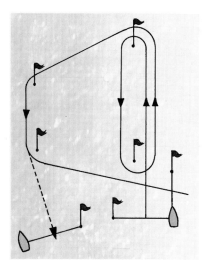

Triangle sausage course

Originally called an Olympic triangle, useful with established classes at open meetings and national events.

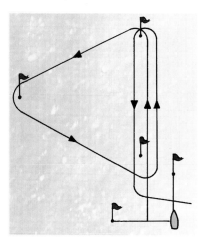

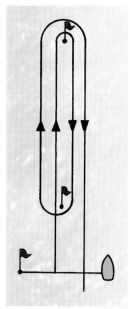

Sausage or windward/leeward course

Very popular with modern asymmetric boats, as they have to go downwind in a series of broad reaches for maximum speed.

Starting sequence

The starting system used by the majority of sailing clubs consists of a warning signal, a preparatory signal and a start signal. The flags and sound signals used to draw attention to the starting sequence are shown in G12, the RYA Advanced Handbook. The most common system is 5 minute - 4 minute - 1 minute - go.

Other signals relating to starting

Individual Recall

If one or more competitors are over the line at the start then flag X (blue cross against white background) will be displayed immediately after the start with a sound signal. This will be displayed until all competitors have started properly, or up to 4 minutes after the start, or up to 1 minute before a following start.

General Recall

If several unidentified boats are over the line at the start then the race will be restarted to ensure fairness. Under these circumstances the First Substitute flag (Yellow triangle on a blue triangular background) will be flown with 2 sound signals. The preparatory signal for the next start will normally be 1 minute after the First Substitute is lowered.

Starting Penalty Flags

The starting penalty flags are displayed with the preparatory flags and dropped 1 minute before the start. If any one of these flags is flown then a boat that enters the triangle formed by the two ends of the start line and the first buoy will be penalised as follows:

Flag I - the competitor must sail to the pre-start side of the line by going around either end of the line.

Flag Z - the competitor shall receive a 20% scoring penalty.

Black Flag - the competitor shall be disqualified and shall not be allowed to restart the race if a general recall is necessary.

Boat Tuning

Tuning a boat can vary between knowing when to ease the kicking strap or pull on the Cunningham in a Laser, to adjusting mast rake and altering the spreaders in a Fireball. The best place to start tuning is to find out what other people who race successfully in the class are doing. Most class associations and sail makers publish tuning guides. Class websites are a good place to start.

Before experimenting with any rig settings on a boat it is a good idea to set it up to the class average given in the tuning guides.

Tactics and Strategy

This covers everything from finding the fastest way up the beat using the changes in direction of the wind to manoeuvring at close quarters to gain an advantage on other boats.

Race strategy

Race strategy is the plan you might make depending on the course, the weather, tidal currents, sea state and surrounding land masses.

Tactics

Tactics are the specific techniques used to execute your race strategy. Some of the more common examples of conditions found when racing are shown overleaf. These are just a few examples of tactics around the race course. Others will occur during training and can be looked at as they come up.

Dirty Wind

The wind to leeward of a dinghy is affected in both strength and direction. To continue on the same tack, to leeward and behind another boat, will result in the boat sailing both lower and slower until it has dropped far enough behind to not be affected.

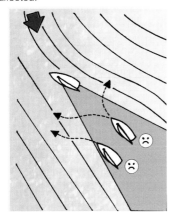

Course down the reach

A tactical advantage can be gained by sailing very low at the start of a reach as long as there is a gap behind you to prevent your wind being blanketed by other boats. This technique allows for a fast approach to the next buoy on the inside of boats which have gone high.

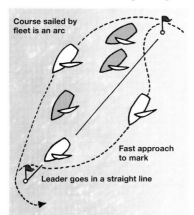

Bear off rapidly round the windward mark. Best done with a gap behind you.
You also approach gybe mark on the inside.

Using Gusts and Lifts and Avoiding Headers

By studying the water upwind whilst beating, gusts can be seen as dark areas on the water. Advantages can be gained by preparing the boat for the gusts and altering course to make the best use of them. The wind is constantly changing in direction so one tack will always point a dinghy slightly closer to the next mark than the other - this is the lifted tack.

Wind bends

Where the wind bends there can be a significant advantage in sailing towards the inside of the bend. This should result in the boat sailing a shorter distance, as it will spend more time on a lifted tack

Sail towards the centre of a wind bend

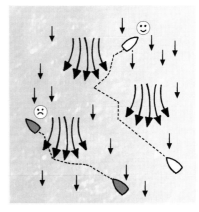

Wind bend around headland

Wind bend off land

Boat Handling

To be able to apply tactics around the race course good boat handling skills are essential. There are many exercises which concentrate specifically on boat handling including tacking/gybing on the whistle, follow my leader, slalom courses and racing around a very tight course.

Using a video camera to help with coaching can help speed up the learning process.

It is generally accepted that to develop boat handling skills it is important to break down a particular manoeuvre into smaller segments. This enables the sailor to focus on particular areas of improvement. Remember you can't eat an elephant whole.

Simple Rules

As well as port/starboard and windward/leeward rules we need to add a few more useful rules when we are racing.

Overtaking

The generalisation of overtaking boat keeps clear does have some limitations. The main one being that if the boats are on opposite tack, as often happens on downwind legs, then the boat on port must keep clear.

Mark Rounding

If boat A has on overlap with boat B when either of the two boats reaches the two length zone then boat B shall allow room for boat A to pass the mark.

This applies even if the overlap is subsequently broken. Boat A has no rights if an overlap is gained inside the two-length zone.

The two-length zone is defined as an imaginary circle with a radius equivalent to twice the hull length of the boat concerned, centered on the mark.

Tacking and Gybing

When a boat is tacking or gybing it has no right of way and must keep clear of all other boats.

If after completing a tack or gybe it gains a right of way over another boat, the other boat must have opportunity to keep clear after the completion of the tack or gybe.

Room to keep clear

If a right of way boat changes course she must give the other boat room to keep clear.

Penalties

A boat infringing a rule may exonerate itself by taking a penalty. The penalty is to turn the boat through 720° in the same direction at the earliest opportunity. The boat shall have no rights of way during the manoeuvre.

If a boat fouls a mark she may exonerate herself by performing a 360° turn at the earliest opportunity.

It should be noted that both of these penalties are routinely altered by the Sailing Instructions.

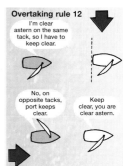

Overtaking rule 12

I'm clear astern on the same tack, so I have to keep clear.

No, on opposite tacks, port keeps clear.

Keep clear, you are clear astern.

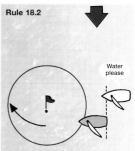

Rule 18.2

Water please

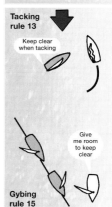

Tacking rule 13

Keep clear when tacking

Give me room to keep clear

Gybing rule 15

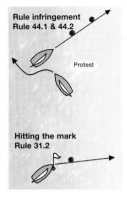

Practical Racing and exercises

By far the most important aspect of teaching people to race is actually racing on the water. Many different exercises can be used to develop sailors understanding and performance around a course. The race can be broken down as follows and specific exercises used to improve performance.

Starting

Starting is a key skill and confidence on the start line is essential if racing is to be enjoyed successfully. Starting exercises should receive major emphasis during a 'Start Racing' Course.

Timing to hit line at start

A simple start line and a short windward leg can be used to practice a number of starts with a short race afterwards. For the purpose of training a shortened 2 minute - 1 minute - go is normally used.

Holding position and accelerating

Again a simple start line and windward leg can be used, but the start sequence should involve the start being sounded 15 seconds or so either side of the normal start signal. This encourages people to practice holding position near the start line and accelerating away at the start signal. One of the problems in training with a small number of dinghies is that the starts are not very realistic - there is rarely congestion at the start line.

Another useful exercise is 'Follow my leader', taking the boats on a close reach and slowing down almost to a standstill before accelerating again.

Line bias

To raise awareness of the line bias the anchor rope on the committee boat can be periodically lengthened and shortened between starts to alter the bias. This will encourage sailors to regularly check the bias of the start line.

Windward leg
Speed upwind

Tacking on the whistle is a very useful exercise to focus on upwind speed. Start the sailors out in a 'Follow-my-leader' formation and brief them to go close hauled at a given signal. This should start all the boats going upwind, level and in clear air. The boats can either carry on for a long period without tacking to practice speed and pointing, or they can do a series of tacks on the whistle to practice boat handling. When the boats spread out too far start the exercise again.

Tactics and lay lines

After a briefing on tactics a number of short races can be run with a finish between the safety boat and the windward mark. Boats should be encouraged to practice tacking on the lay line and covering other boats up the beat whilst protecting their clear air.

Mark rounding

Practice bearing away

A small triangular or sausage course should be laid with all the boats sailing around it. The safety boat can then be held near the windward mark to offer coaching advice to the boats bearing away. The emphasis will be on keeping the boats level or leaning to windward slightly, easing the kicking strap, moving crew weight back if it is blowing and where possible raising the centreboard.

Practice gybing

A slalom course can be used to practice reach to reach gybing or a whistle to initiate run-to-run gybing.

Tactics

Start the boats at the windward mark of a triangular course, enabling the boats to arrive at the gybe mark close together. This should allow sailors a chance to think ahead and practice good mark rounding. The safety boat should ideally be positioned inside the course near the gybe mark.

Offwind legs

Speed including spinnakers if applicable

Start the boats from 'Follow-my-leader' on a beam reach, a good distance upwind of a mark. This will allow the boats an equal start with other boats in close proximity. Focus should be on boat speed alone with the boats not attempting to block the wind of others.

Tactics

A similar exercise can be run but this time with the emphasis on gaining position by covering other boats whilst keeping their own air clear. This can be done on a reach or a run.

The RYA Portsmouth Yardstick Scheme

The RYA Portsmouth Yardstick Scheme is operated jointly by the RYA and the clubs to quantify the performance of different class boats, enabling them to race against each other on level terms.

The measure of performance is the Portsmouth Number (PN), expressed as whole numbers from 600 to 1700. The ratio between two PNs reflects the difference in performance. Assuming *Nervous Wreck* has a PN of 700 and *Late Starter* one of 1400, if *Nervous Wreck* completes a race in 70 minutes then, for *Late Starter* to beat her on Corrected Time, she has to finish the race in under 140 minutes.

To establish a PN for a new class of boat it is necessary for a boat of that class to race against boats with well established PNs (classified as Yardsticks) against which the assessment of the new class can be made. This is done over a period of time until the PN becomes stable.

Each year the RYA circulates all clubs with a questionnaire requesting details of their assessments. The lists of Portsmouth Numbers are based on this data and published in the RYA book YR2 and on the RYA web site: www.rya.org.uk. This booklet also gives full recommendations on the use of the Scheme and is a must for any club running yardstick races.

There are many methods of applying the Scheme at club level as detailed in YR2 but the most popular of these are the conventional Portsmouth Yardstick Scheme race and the Pursuit Race.

In the former all boats start at the same time, sail the same course and finish on the same finish line. The race result is then determined by calculating a Corrected Time (C) for each boat by the formula C=1000xE/PN where E is the elapsed time i.e. the time it took for the boat to complete the race. The boat with the shortest C wins.

With the most common form of Pursuit Races each class of boat starts at a different, pre-determined, time with the slowest starting first and the fastest last. All boats sail the same course for a set time. The order of the boats when that time expires gives the race result. The different start times are calculated from the PN of each class and the desired start time for the race.

Simple examples of the calculations for both of these types of race are given below.

Handicap Race

Start all boats at the same time, make them sail the same distance and record their finishing times. A simple formula can then be used to give all the boats a corrected time.

Pursuit Race

Start all boats at different times with the slow boats going first and make them sail for a predetermined period. This has the advantage that boats know how they have finished in the race - the first boat to finish is the winner. Some compromise is unavoidable because the start times have to be rounded to the nearest 30 seconds.

Calculations
Conventional PYS Race

For example if an RS 400 finished in 42 minutes 30 secs, a Laser finished the race in 45 minutes 30 secs and a Wayfarer finished in 46 minutes 9 secs.

The corrected time for the RS 400 (PN 952) would be;

Elapsed time in secs 42 minutes 30 secs = (42 x 60) + 30 secs = 2550 secs

Corrected time $\quad \dfrac{2550}{952}$ x 1000 = 2679 secs = 44 minutes 39 secs

The corrected time for the Laser (PN 1078) would be;

Elapsed time in secs 45 minutes 30 secs = (45 x 60) + 30 secs = 2730 secs

Corrected time $\quad \dfrac{2730}{1078}$ x 1000 = 2532 secs = 42 minutes 12 secs

The corrected time for the Wayfarer (PN1099) would be;

Elapsed time in secs 46 minutes 9 secs = (46 x 60) + 9 secs = 2769 secs

Corrected time $\quad \dfrac{2769}{1099}$ x 1000 = 2519 secs = 41 minutes 59 secs

Therefore even though the Wayfarer finished last on the water it actually beat the Laser and the RS 400 on corrected time.

Pursuit Race

To calculate the start times for a race between a Laser, a Wayfarer and an RS400 the calculation would be as follows.

We need to decide how long we want the slowest boat to be racing for; in this example we will have the Wayfarer racing for an hour (60 minutes).

Next we need to decide how long it would take the other boats to sail the same distance as the Wayfarer.

$$\frac{1099(\text{Wayfarer PN})}{60\text{minutes}} = \frac{1078(\text{Laser PN})}{?\text{minutes}}$$

This is the same as saying $\frac{1078}{(1099 \div 60)}$ = Laser racing time in minutes = 58.85 minutes

which rounds up to= 59 minutes

Therefore the Laser would start 1 minute after the Wayfarer.

For the RS400 $\frac{952}{(1099/60)}$ = RS400 racing time in minutes = 51.97 minutes

which rounds up to = 52 minutes

Therefore the RS400 would start 8 minutes after the Wayfarer.

If the race started at 1000 then the Laser would start at 1001 and the RS400 would start at 1008. The race needs to finish at or as near as possible to 1100.

KEELBOAT INSTRUCTOR TRAINING

The National Sailing Scheme can be delivered in keelboats by the following

- A Keelboat Instructor qualified through a 5-day keelboat instructor training course

- A Senior Instructor with a Day Skipper practical certificate or higher

- A Yachtmaster Instructor

- A Dinghy/Multihull Instructor with a two-day keelboat instructor conversion course.

Generally, the Principal or Chief Instructor of a Centre teaching in keelboats will be a Senior Instructor with a Keelboat Instructor endorsement, or a Yachtmaster Instructor.

Performance Sailing in keelboats should be run by any of the above with an Advanced Instructor endorsement.

Instructing in keelboats

The 'method' progression of learning to sail can be successfully taught in keelboats with a few simple modifications. Land drills are inappropriate, but the use of the boat controls for tacking and gybing can be demonstrated on a mooring.

The main differences from teaching in a dinghy are:

- The instructor will probably be teaching on board rather than in a rescue boat

- Allow students to take control if they are competent and avoid standing over them at the backstay

- There are only four essentials

- Techniques for grounding recovery

- Use of engine

- Man overboard technique

- Use of harnesses

With up to five students on board there is less helming time per person, although the crewing tasks are more involved. Move everyone around regularly. Little and often is appropriate for boat handling. For example the group can practise picking up moorings by approaching on the correct point of sail without actually securing to the buoy. This allows you to teach the principles and gives everyone a try quickly, allowing for slight mis-judgements.

Man overboard

Small keelboats can use the dinghy method but for larger boats (where a man held in the water will not effect the drift of the boat) use one or both of the following:

Quick stop with engine:

- Man overboard

- Pointer allocated immediate heave to

- Drop lifebelt and Dan buoy
- Start engine, check no ropes overboard
- Drop jib in hove to position
- Motor sail downwind until wind indicator points at man
- Motor upwind
- Retrieve man at shrouds keeping propeller clear

Reach-tack-reach man overboard

- Pointer allocated
- Immediate heave to
- Drop lifebelt and Dan buoy
- Sail away 10 -15 boat lengths on apparent beam reach
- Tack - can drop jib
- Point boat at MOB
- Ensure main can flap, if not dip downwind
- Spill and fill main on close reach aiming slightly upwind
- Retrieve MOB on leeward side

Retrieval of MOB

With larger keelboats you need to have a method of retrieving people from the water. If they are conscious and not hypothermic use a ladder or foothold, e.g. bowline. Otherwise consider:

- Boarding ladder
- Detached mainsheet
- Handy Billy from boom or halyard
- Parbuckling with small sail
- Dinghy
- Helicopter harness or equivalent

Handling under power

- At Level 2 keep the power manoeuvres to simple alongsides and moorings
- Demonstrate prop wash effect by engaging astern while secured alongside
- Practise turning boat under power
- Prepare for alongside - observe wind and tide, fenders and warps, position crew, communication, boat control, secure, use of springs

Moorings

- Wind and tide
- Preparation (boat hook/warp)
- Communication
- Boat control

Seamanship Skills Keelboat

Grounding

- Lee shore dangers
- Awareness of state of tide

If grounding on windward side:

- Ease or drop main, back jib, heel

If grounding on lee shore:

- If quick you may be able to sheet in main and tack off
- If not, drop main quickly to avoid being blown on further
- If you have an engine heel boat and motor off
- With no engine, put out kedge
- If the tide is falling and no help is available, protect side of boat as it dries

Emergency steering

Keelboats can be steered rudderless by lashing the helm exactly amidships and using sail trim and, to some extent, balance as in a dinghy. Emergency steering can involve the use of an oar, a spinnaker pole or boathook, or even a bucket attached to each quarter.

Day Sailing keelboat

One day of a Day Sailing Course should be spent undertaking a day passage. Your planning must be first class. The Senior Instructor or Keelboat Instructor is responsible for the safety of the whole group and should not hesitate to change or abandon the plan if weather or other circumstances dictate.

When planning a trip consider the following:

- Weather
- Distance
- Student preparation - laminated chartlets, notebook
- Tides, streams, tidal gates, heights for entering and leaving harbours or anchorages
- Extra clothing, drink, food
- Extra equipment, tow lines, flares
- Radio contact, shore contact
- Emergency plan, refuge port
- Danger on route, shipping etc.
- Landmarks on route, buoys etc.
- Moorings, pontoon, anchorage at destination

The problem is to give everyone an experience of pilotage rather than following the boat in front. Try to encourage everyone to become involved in the pilotage but avoid splitting the fleet unless there is an instructor in each boat.

MULTIHULL INSTRUCTOR TRAINING

Multihull instructor courses are open to candidates with the appropriate standard of multihull sailing ability. This is confirmed by a practical test identical to the pre-entry assessment outlined on page 49 with the exception that the rudderless sailing is omitted.

The instructor course itself has a similar format to that for dinghy instructors, with the exception that many of the boat handling techniques are different. Candidates are assessed by a specialist Coach/Assessor and if successful, are qualified as RYA Multihull Instructors.

Existing RYA Dinghy Instructors with the relevant multihull experience, who wish to gain a Multihull endorsement to their instructor certificate may do so by taking a two-day endorsement course. This will include the pre-entry test outlined above and training and assessment in practical multihull teaching techniques.

As the Dart 16 is the multihull class most widely used by RYA training centres, the notes which follow are aimed particularly at that class. Instructors teaching in other classes may wish to modify the techniques as appropriate.

Outline teaching method/Notes for Multihulls

Clothing/gear collection

- As for monohulls

Rigging/Launching

- Show students where to sit
- Demonstrate which items may be used as handholds, and which must not be used
- Hoist mainsail first
- Boat must be head to wind to hook on halyard lock
- Tack downhaul must not be tensioned yet, nor mainsheet attached
- Hoist jib and reeve jib sheets
- Attach rudders and lock up
- Lift bow and slide trolley under
- Show students how to hold onto the boat, with one hand on the forestay bridle, the other holding the bow
- Trolley boat into water and float off
- Stow trolley ashore
- Warn students of danger of placing feet under hulls in shallow water
- Crew holds boat head to wind as outlined above
- Helmsman attaches mainsheet

- Leave windward shore by sailing backwards; crew on each hull between bridle and main beam to lift sterns clear
- Control rate and direction of sternway by backing jib
- Leave other shores by sailing off gently, lowering windward rudder first
- When in clear water, stop to lower leeward rudder and tension tack downhaul

Coming ashore

- Lift the leeward rudder first
- Ease mainsail tack downhaul
- Sail in slowly with the traveller eased off
- Crew sits on main beam and chooses right moment to slide off into the water on windward side to hold boat
- Meanwhile, helmsman lifts windward rudder when close to shore
- With an onshore wind the crew can dangle his legs in the water on the windward side, forward of the shroud to slow the boat down
- In strong winds with restricted access, boat is sailed in under jib alone

Coming ashore on sandy beaches with an onshore wind and large waves, the technique is different:

- De-power the mainsail
- Pick the right area and both helmsman and crew sit aft to keep the bows up
- At the right moment the helmsman trips the rudders and keeps going straight for the shore
- Take care when alighting from the boat and turning it head to wind
- Basic instruction from pebble beaches is not recommended

Familiarisation/joyride

- As for monohulls
- You should ensure that the trampoline is tight to give a greater feeling of security
- In light winds it is possible to have a 2:1 student: instructor ratio but above force 3 the ratio should be 1:1 to avoid putting undue loads on the rig

Orientation/Basic boat controls

Orientation is as for monohulls, but there are important differences in the basic boat controls session:

- Point out that multihulls do have brakes - the rudders
- The mainsail/jib controls used for monohull teaching are ineffective for multihulls
- Introduce two traveller positions: upwind/reaching and downwind
- The centreboard demonstration is generally inappropriate

Going about

The teaching of successful tacking relies on two essential and related teaching points - maintaining sufficient boat speed and sailing an efficient course to windward prior to tacking i.e. neither pinching nor close-reaching. It follows that it is not practical to tack from reach to reach so the existence of the No-Go-Zone must be introduced earlier than in monohull teaching.

The use of colour coded sheets and traveller can be a considerable advantage for beginners to avoid confusion. The tacking drill below includes the use of trapeze although this might not be appropriate for the very early stages of instruction. Having said that, it is essential that proper boat speed and course be maintained into the tack.

The basic manoeuvre is:

- Helmsman checks inside and around boat, especially area into which he is going to sail, says 'ready about'

- Crew comes in off trapeze (if used) and unhooks harness and shouts 'Ready'

- Helmsman pushes tiller extension slowly and firmly until the tillers are at about 45 degrees to their normal position and holds tiller extension in that position

- Crew and helmsman both wait until the jib starts to cross the boat

- Helmsman then moves to a kneeling position on the centreline of the boat, facing aft

- He eases the mainsheet by about 15cm and clears the sheet. Crew eases jib sheet and moves to centreline.

- Helmsman passes the tiller extension behind the mainsheet and crosses to the new windward side, picking up the mainsheet and un-cleating it

- As the battens 'crack', helmsman takes up his new position, centres the tillers and trims he mainsheet. (In light winds, the helmsman needs to assist the sail to take up its new shape.)

- Crew then balances the boat as appropriate and trims the jib.

The main teaching points about tacking a multihull are:

- The time it takes

- Avoiding the temptation to slow down or pinch immediately before tacking.

- This might mean the crew staying out on the trapeze until the helmsman initiates the tack

- Overcoming the tendency to centralise the tillers too early

- Ensuring that the student does not let go of the extension

- The importance of trimming the mainsheet both before and during the tack. This means keeping the power on before starting a tack but remembering to ease the sheet as outlined above. In light winds, it will be impossible for the helmsman to reverse the mainsail camber when tacking by snatching the mainsheet falls unless he has eased the sheet prior to tacking.

Going about practice/sailing to windward

- As for monohulls, except that it is not practical to tack from reach to reach.

The five essentials:

1 **Sail setting** - the use of telltales nearest the head of each sail is introduced earlier than in monohull teaching, because of the fully battened mainsail. Introduce the use of the streamer on the forestay bridle as an aid downwind (the streamer should be at 90 degrees to the boat for optimum downwind sailing).

2 **Balance** - stress the different helmsman/crew positions for light and medium winds.

3 **Trim** - check that the boat is level by comparing waterlines forward and aft.

4 **Centreboard** - inappropriate for Darts. Other multihulls may have centreboards used in

the same way as in monohulls. Downwind gybing may require small amounts of centreboard for steerage.

5 **Course sailed** - as for monohulls but emphasise the amount of time lost through inefficient tacking. Also stress the importance of gybing downwind.

Downwind sailing/gybing

The basic manoeuvre is:

- Helmsman sails on optimum downwind course (streamer at 90 degrees to boat) and checks around him, particularly the area into which he is going to turn
- Calls 'stand by to gybe'
- Crew checks area, replies 'ready' and moves to centreline of boat, picking up new jib sheet.
- Helmsman says 'gybe oh', pulling tiller extension steadily towards him until tillers are at 45 degrees to centreline. He moves to a kneeling position facing aft, close to the centreline
- Crew kneels on centreline, crouching low and facing forward (possibly holding onto toestraps)
- Helmsman lifts tiller extension and swings it abaft mainsheet falls, pulling the falls towards him with it
- Helmsman changes hands on tiller extension by passing forward hand forward of falls and grasping extension with it
- Aft hand is used to cushion speed of gybe by catching falls of mainsheet. The inertia of that movement is used to swing the body to face the old sitting position
- Crew stays in position, keeping low
- Helmsman resumes normal position for new course
- Crew resumes correct position for prevailing wind and next course

The main teaching points about gybing a multihull are:

- Students should not try to centralise the tiller in the middle of the gybe, as for monohull sailing
- Beginners should be discouraged from using the tiller bar, rather than the extension
- You must make students aware of the large area needed to gybe a multihull, particularly by beginners
- Ensure that slack mainsheet and traveller line are left on the centreline of the boat by the rear beam before gybing, to avoid kneeling on them and hence restricting their movement

Further sessions

The ability to sail around a triangular course marks an important stage in basic instruction, as it shows that the student can tackle all points of sailing.

Teaching of man overboard recovery differs fundamentally from monohull teaching. Having regained control, the person left aboard will prefer to gybe rather than tack to get back to the man in the water, as it is quicker and the helmsman is in control throughout the manoeuvre. In addition, the man is recovered from between the hulls and if necessary over the main beam, rather than at the shroud.

Capsize recovery drill

The golden rule about staying with the boat is more important with multihulls due to their high speed of drift when capsized in strong winds.

The basic routine for recovery is

- Helmsman and crew climb onto lower hull
- Crew moves forward to 'anchor' the bow in the water whilst helmsman moves aft to free the mainsheet and traveller line
- Helmsman moves forward again to grasp jib sheet or righting line. Bow/mast allowed to swing into wind
- Crew leans out on sheet to right boat
- As it comes upright, helmsman grabs handles on bottom of trampoline to prevent a second capsize
- Helmsman and crew board via rear beam

In the case of total inversion

- Helmsman and crew move to transom and board there
- Helmsman ensures that mainsheet and traveller have been eased
- Crew retrieves jib sheet from windward side
- Both sit on leeward quarter to sink it and then start righting manoeuvre

The main teaching points are to encourage beginners to use the handholds and to emphasise that even with comparatively little righting moment, capsize recovery is possible.

Teaching further skills

Once the basic techniques have been covered in RYA Level 1 and 2 courses, further multihull training follows the syllabi laid down in the RYA National Sailing Scheme Logbook G4, amended as appropriate with specialist techniques.

SENIOR INSTRUCTOR TRAINING

The Principal of an RYA Training Centre carries the formal responsibility for ensuring that all training complies with RYA guidelines, laid down in the current *Guidance Notes for inspection of RYA recognised Training Centres*. The Principal may himself be a Senior Instructor or may appoint a Senior Instructor to act as sailing manager, and to ensure that sailing tuition is organised according to RYA methods and standards.

The qualities required of a Senior Instructor are patience, resourcefulness, and the ability to deal with students and instructors. SIs should also have the organisational ability to ensure that courses are enjoyable, safe and informative.

Quite apart from his responsibility to his students, the Senior Instructor has a responsibility to his instructors, to his club or employer and the RYA.

Senior Instructor training is a combination of teaching and work experience. Courses are organised on a regional basis with minimum numbers in order to bring together candidates with a variety of backgrounds and instructing experience.

The course may be split into two weekends or a number of days, with the separate sessions being run at different centres within a region. This gives candidates the opportunity of working at different places and hence being introduced to different operational problems.

As the SI course may be the last formal course which most instructors attend, it aims to cover as many of their needs as possible, it is impossible to do this by didactic or dictatorial teaching. Instead, SI training and assessment consists of a mixture of discussion and task-related projects, together with short specialist inputs on specific subjects, either from Coaches running the course or from course members themselves.

The course should be informative and energising. Each practical session will be run by one of the course candidates and will form part of the continuous assessment of the course. The candidate will be expected to plan and organise the session, brief the other candidates, run the exercise and then debrief the group. In this way all candidates will experience a range of short, high-energy sessions on a variety of topics and in a variety of styles.

The Coach/Assessor will then debrief the whole group on the way the session was managed, so that every candidate will learn group control techniques by experience. In addition, the actual exercises used will be chosen to benefit the other course members who are participating in them. Such practical sessions could cover any part of the National Sailing Scheme and thus provide a good opportunity for candidates to refresh and improve their own skills.

The Senior Instructor will be capable of managing and supervising one or more groups afloat, each group taught by an appropriately qualified instructor.

The Senior Instructor will also understand the full requirements of RYA Training Centre Recognition and where necessary put in place all the necessary systems and documentation. This may well include carrying out or revising a risk assessment and specifying and recording safety procedures.

Coastal Senior Instructor courses will include training in the delivery of the Day Sailing course. Candidates are referred to the notes on page 79. Careful planning, group control, appropriate safety cover and constant awareness are vital for safe day trips from coastal venues. Candidates will receive input and be expected to demonstrate these qualities during the course.

Course planning

Parts of the SI course cover topics relevant to all courses. Others are specific to certain levels. The general topics can be considered by following the framework:

Anatomy of the Club Course

1. Regional coach approves course. Decide costing.

2. Confirm course with venue(s) regarding use of facilities. Confirm liabilities and insurance

3. Advertise course. Distribute booking forms or similar

4. Receive bookings, issue receipts/acknowledgments/acceptances and home study material.

5. Plan theory programme, assess instructor and audio/visual input
   Order RYA publications

6. Send out joining instructions

7. Send out letters asking for instructor help

8. Match available boats to instructors and students. Establish need for extra boats and equipment

9. Make arrangements for teaching and safety boats and drivers

10. Arrange for Assessor if appropriate

11. Compile register and progress chart

12. Pre-course briefing for students

13. Start of course briefing for instructors

14. Consultation sessions with instructors

15. Debriefing at end of each session if possible

16. Formal conclusion of course (award of certificates)

17. Indication of students to follow-up

18. Thanks to instructors, helpers, venue(s)

19. Course evaluation - feedback from students and instructors

20. Final costing

Course Organisation

The most important part of the Senior Instructor's role is day-to-day organisation of each course. Every course has four elements - the students, the instructors, the fleet/teaching facilities and the syllabus. It is the task of the Senior Instructor to ensure that they all fit together harmoniously. Apart from those caused by deteriorating weather conditions, problems usually arise from poor planning or a lack of communication between the SI, instructors and students.

The SI is responsible for instructor/student ratios and matching. Be prepared to change crews or instructors if necessary, avoid the classic miss-matches of students, such as father/son or wife/husband. The SI is also responsible for group control ashore and afloat.

Most teaching centres have house rules' about gear stowage, how boats are to be left and slipway procedures. Ensure that all your instructors (including temporary staff) know them.

Similarly, the SI is responsible for ensuring that all the students on a course are learning the right things at the right pace. One tactful way of ensuring, for example, that all your helpers follow the same techniques when teaching tacking and gybing is for the SI to give the first land drill demonstration.

Group control afloat is covered in some detail in the chapter on single-handers on page 67, but in addition the SI is responsible for the provision of safety cover for the fleet. In many teaching centres the distinction between teaching boats and safety boats is blurred, so you must ensure that each instructor realises the scope of his responsibilities.

In some cases and in some weather conditions the availability of safety cover will dictate or limit the scope of teaching, which in turn means that the SI is responsible for an alternative programme if the group cannot get afloat.

At the other extreme, the SI must try to continue effective teaching if there is too little wind, in extreme cases postponing part of the course to a later date. At all times, the SI must be able to recognise what is going on in the teaching fleet, either from a safety boat or from the shore, so that problems can be anticipated and avoided.

Before each practical session, the SI must be confident that each of his instructors has a clear idea of the aim of that session, so that they can confirm that the aims have been met during the debriefing.

It should already be clear that as an SI you have a great deal of responsibility, relying on your resourcefulness to solve problems as they arise. Apart from directing the work of your instructors, you also have to assist and support them, particularly when they turn to you for advice. The following summary of brief questions might provoke further thoughts. How would you answer them?

Ten questions from instructors

1. One of my students is learning far more quickly that the others. What do I do?
2. It's blowing Force 5 out there, what do I do? (Day 2 of a beginner's course)
3. What should I do with my hands when I'm lecturing?
4. You've asked me in to cover for Robin whilst he's away, how do I know what his students have covered so far? (Third day of a Seamanship course)
5. How do I tell when my students are ready to move on to the next stage of the syllabus?
6. Bob and Sally say they're too old to take part in the capsize drill. What can I tell them?
7. What do I do if three of my Toppers capsize at once?
8. Why should I shave? (From a 22-year-old male instructor)
9. Why should I bother with the kill cord on the outboard? It only gets in the way
10. How do I teach Jenny to sail? She's only got one hand.

You could be forgiven for thinking that some of those questions should never arise, but the fact is that your instructors will always look to you for advice. Even though they should know the answers, you must treat questions from instructors in just the same way that they should treat questions from students.

Catastrophe Clinic

One of the advantages of a large Senior Instructor course is that it brings together candidates with a wide, varied collective experience of teaching sailing. One useful way of sharing that experience is by the exercise known as Catastrophe Clinic.

Each candidate writes a short outline of the worst things which have happened to them whilst teaching sailing. The outline should contain details of:

The type of venue (inland, estuary, open sea)

The size of fleet and type of boats

The number of students and the level of course

The number of instructors and teaching or rescue boats

What happened

The group leader then collects all the examples and introduces them one by one for group discussion, with the author of each scenario remaining silent when his 'catastrophe' is discussed. After the group has discussed the problem and decided what they would have done in the circumstances, the author then explains what he actually did and why.

Some problems may result from the unexpected behaviour of instructors or students and will call upon the SI's resources of tact and diplomacy in finding a solution.

The real epics usually result from not one single problem but a string of circumstances, each one of which on its own might not have been so serious. The horror of multiple capsizes in deteriorating weather conditions, possibly with dangerous lee shore or commercial shipping nearby, calls for clear thinking to establish priorities and act decisively. The two Golden Rules in such circumstances are:

- Count heads

- Save people before property

One recurring theme, which is not highlighted above, is that of the student with a health problem, either unknown or undisclosed. Examples range from the teenage diabetic on a residential course who forgets his medication in the excitement of the activity, to the middle aged man who suffers a suspected heart attack during a capsize recovery session and the woman who collapses in the hot shower after sailing, for reasons totally unconnected with the activity.

All have specific lessons for the Senior Instructor but the overall message is that the SI in control of the group must know of any health problems. The usual way of finding out is to require all students to complete a health declaration. As outlined on page 9.

Session Planning Exercises

Before attending the training course, candidates will complete a home study pack from the RYA. This will be sent to candidates in advance by course organisers. Material in this pack will include exercises on risk assessments and operating procedures, as well as session planning and delivery. The pack should be completed by all candidates for discussion or presentation during the course.

Senior Instructor Assessment

Throughout your SI Course you will be assessed on your ability to plan, organise and run practical sessions, and on your input to shore based sessions. In particular, the course organiser is looking for:

- Aims clearly stated (did the session have clear objectives?)

- Briefing was complete and clear (did the group know what was required)?

- Sailing area identified

- The leader could be clearly identified

- The whole group was involved
- Enthusiasm was maintained
- Problems were solved
- Signals (two way) were established including Abandon
- On-water coaching took place
- Group control was maintained (no unnecessary delays) ashore and afloat
- The clients were carefully debriefed and problems discussed and solved
- Session achieved all objectives.
- Clients' questions were answered
- Clients were informed of their successes. The follow-on session was described
- The equipment was carefully put away after the session

Good relationships with others

In addition, the course organiser will be applying an assessment based on his experience of the RYA Coaching Scheme to decide whether you meet the requirements of a Senior Instructor as defined on page 19. If he is unable to confirm that you have successfully completed the course, the Coach will outline the reasons for that decision and an action plan needed for future success.

COACH/ASSESSOR TRAINING

Coach/Assessor Appointment

Experienced Senior Instructors are appointed by the National Coach as Coach/Assessors to train Instructors. This appointment is renewable annually, subject to the completion of an update every 5 years.

Coach/Assessor Training

The RYA is always looking for good Senior Instructors to train and appoint as Coach/Assessors. The primary function of the Coach/Assessor is training instructors, but Coach/Assessors also inspect RYA Training Centres following a further training day. Experienced Senior Instructors interested in Coach/Assessor training should approach their Regional Coach to discuss the possibility of their names being put forward for training.

Selection and Training is therefore a three stage process:

1. Candidates are put forward by the Regional Coach and accepted by RYA HQ

2. Selection and Preparation Course

3. Training Course

Instructor training can be a challenging experience for candidates. The RYA requires Coach/Assessors with sensitivity to individuals' needs, coupled with the ability to be strong role models. Enthusiasm and a commitment to the values and methodology of the Scheme are essential, as are an approachable and friendly attitude.

During selection candidates:

- Demonstrate any part of the National Sailing Scheme to a good standard in tidal conditions, including the use of modern designs of boat

- Demonstrate the ability to teach any part of the Scheme

- Demonstrate the provision of good feedback and coaching on any part of the National Sailing Scheme

- Demonstrate very good communication skills throughout

The training course itself includes training and assessment in briefing and debriefing instructor candidates, sailing and coaching in high performance boats and input on a number of topics relevant to the role of the Coach/Assessor.

Training Instructors

Instructors teaching sailing follow the process of brief-task-debrief (page 22), with the task being a sailing skill. Instructor courses follow the same principle except that the task is teaching. The problem for the Coach/Assessor running an instructor course is organising teaching sessions, which are as real as possible.

The trainee instructor can practise teaching to either

a) the fellow trainees,

b) the Coach/Assessor, or

c) real beginners.

The presence of the Coach/Assessor is always going to affect the relationship between instructor and pupil but a skillful Coach/Assessor can minimise nervousness and the false nature of the situation. While 'real' students are a useful part of the instructor training course, these volunteers can only realistically be arranged for a limited number of sessions. Also, from the viewpoint of the beginners, the instruction can be rather disjointed and possibly delivered by an instructor who is far from expert.

Debriefing instructors

When debriefing, avoid having a conversation about sailing. The Coach/Assessor must concentrate on the delivery of the instruction. The section of this book on keeping students informed (page 28) is particularly relevant on instructor courses.

Organising an instructor course

- Obtain the consent of the Regional Coach and inform RYA HQ
- Ensure candidates are aware of the eligibility requirements including the pre-sailing test
- Arrange for a second Coach/Assessor on the final day. The course is five days minimum and the moderation should be on the last day
- The teaching ratio is 6 trainee instructors to 1 Coach/Assessor, with a second Coach/Assessor on the final day

The training course

A typical course might spend about 1 to 2 days on the Method and Level 1 and 2, and a day in single-handers including racing. The remaining time would be spent on seamanship teaching and spinnakers and high performance dinghies if available. The final moderation day draws together all elements of the course.

Assessing instructors

The instructor course is much harder to assess than a sailing course because good and bad teaching is dependent to some extent upon personality as well as presentation skills. For example Coach/Assessors can be faced by technically good sailors who have problems relating well to students, become aggressive or anxious or show other traits, making them unsuitable as instructors. Coach/Assessors are not qualified to assess personality and should take the view that instructors are doing their best to do well but might need assistance in teaching skills. If at the end of the course the Coach/Assessor has strong reservations about a trainee instructor's suitability to do the job, the debrief should be restricted to communication and teaching skills rather than a character assassination. The second Coach/Assessor is invaluable here and prevents a personality clash influencing the overall result.

Unsuccessful candidates should be given an action plan. If the problem is a poor rapport with students, it is safer to require a further training course with assessment by a further two Coach/Assessors.

If a candidate is deferred because of lack of knowledge of a straightforward skill such as the RYA method, they can be re-assessed over a short period by one Coach/Assessor.

Moderation

One of the difficulties of conducting a moderation is that the candidates are likely to be nervous and see the day as a stressful examination rather than an opportunity to demonstrate their teaching skills.

The moderator has to handle this situation carefully, mainly because a nervous candidate can produce the wrong result.

To reduce tension

- Start by giving a reasonably straightforward practical task to teach. If chosen well it should be successful. Say 'well done'. This makes the assessment seem achievable
- Be honest about the intentions of the day. Yes, it is an assessment but there are no tricks and the tasks are chosen to give maximum opportunity to show the skills learnt

- Have an open and honest approach to encourage the candidates to ask if unsure about a task
- Take an interest in the candidate

Tension is increased by

- Being secretive about the test and the tasks
- Lack of communication or prolonged periods of silence
- Self-importance of the Assessor
- Setting unrealistic scenarios
- Quick fire or irrelevant questioning
- Disparaging remarks

The moderator must discuss with the training Coach/Assessor how the day needs to be organised. The training Coach/Assessor can continue the course during the moderation day. Many Coach/Assessors prefer to 'go in cold' with no knowledge of the candidates, whilst others prefer to concentrate on marginal candidates. Either way, the final result must be given by both Coach/Assessors who have discussed each candidate and come to a result which will enhance the RYA training scheme.

NATIONAL VOCATIONAL QUALIFICATIONS FOR DINGHY INSTRUCTORS

The RYA is accredited to train and assess for National Vocational Qualifications at Level 2 in both dinghy and windsurfing instruction. The NVQ Level 2 is roughly equivalent to the standard of the RYA Dinghy Instructor or Windsurfing Level 2 Instructor award. As well as covering the skills required of those courses, the NVQ assessment also covers other skills associated with working at a sailing centre such as contributing to the running of the centre, dealing with clients off the water as well as on, knowledge of health and safety issues etc. These skills are represented by 'units of competence' which make up the qualification:

Unit

D43   Prepare for coaching sessions

D44   Conduct coaching sessions

C35   Deal with accidents and emergencies

D13   Establish and maintain relationships which support the coaching process

B11   Support the development of the sport/activity

As this is a vocational qualification it must be assessed in the candidate's work place and so is most appropriate and easily achievable for instructors already working at a sailing centre, either on a full time or casual basis. There is no requirement for instructors to hold an NVQ.

Anyone wishing to gain an NVQ must complete a portfolio of evidence showing that they have been doing the job of an instructor in a sailing centre with 'real' students, to a satisfactory standard. They will then be assessed and their portfolio will be reviewed to ensure that all areas of the award have been covered. The most common way for an instructor to work towards the NVQ is to complete the RYA instructor course first. The course and the skills learnt on it can then make a large contribution to the candidate's portfolio. It is possible for a candidate to achieve the NVQ without having done the instructor course first. However, it is likely that the process of gathering evidence and being assessed will take considerably longer.

If you would like further information on NVQs in dinghy sailing or windsurfing instruction, please contact the RYA.

NATIONAL SAILING SCHEME INSTRUCTING AND COACHING LOG

DATE	TYPE OF BOAT	HOURS EXPERIENCE		ACTIVITY AND WEATHER CONDITIONS		LOCATION
		Senior Instructor or Coach/ Assessor	Instructor or Racing Coach	Type of Course or Training Programme	Maximum Wind Speed	Centre/Club
Sub totals- hours						

continue overleaf

NATIONAL SAILING SCHEME INSTRUCTING AND COACHING LOG

DATE	TYPE OF BOAT	HOURS EXPERIENCE		ACTIVITY AND WEATHER CONDITIONS		LOCATION
		Senior Instructor or Coach/ Assessor	Instructor or Racing Coach	Type of Course or Training Programme	Maximum Wind Speed	Centre/Club
hours carried forward						
Sub totals hours						

NATIONAL SAILING SCHEME INSTRUCTING AND COACHING LOG

DATE	TYPE OF BOAT	HOURS EXPERIENCE		ACTIVITY AND WEATHER CONDITIONS		LOCATION
		Senior Instructor or Coach/ Assessor	Instructor or Racing Coach	Type of Course or Training Programme	Maximum Wind Speed	Centre/Club
hours carried forward						
Total hours						

RECOMMENDATIONS FOR COACHING AWARDS

ASSISTANT INSTRUCTOR

Training and assessment record   Principal's initials

The candidate:

Is aware of safety requirements

Is aware of teaching sequence used when teaching beginners

Is aware of the teaching points for each part of the sequence

Is proficient in teaching shore drills

Is proficient in teaching capsize recovery

The candidate has demonstrated competence as an Assistant Instructor to the standards laid down by the RYA,

Signed (RYA Principal)

Name in capitals

Recognised Training Centre

Date

RYA DINGHY/KEELBOAT/MULTIHULL/INSTRUCTOR

Eligibility
- Minimum age 16 • Valid first aid certificate • RYA Powerboat Level 2 certificate
- Pre-entry sailing assessment completed in the appropriate type of boat within one year prior to the instructor training course.
- Candidates for a coastal Instructor certificate should undertake the sailing assessment on coastal waters.

Pre-entry Assessment Completed

Venue	COASTAL/INLAND
Date	
Type of boat	DINGHY/KEELBOAT/MULTIHULL
Approved by (RYA Coach/Assessor)	Signature
Name in capitals	

Please note it is also a requirement for instructors to hold a valid first aid certificate of a type approved by the RYA, and a Powerboat Level 2 certificate before progressing to the instructor training course.

Training Course Completed

Venue	COASTAL/INLAND
Date	
Course Organiser (RYA Coach/Assessor)	Signature
Name in capitals	

Assessment/Moderation Completed

I confirm that the candidate has demonstrated competence as an Instructor in a DINGHY/KEELBOAT/MULTIHULL (delete as appropriate) to the standards laid down by the RYA.

Venue COASTAL/INLAND	
Date	
Approved by (RYA Coach/Assessor)	Signature
Name in capitals	

ADVANCED INSTRUCTOR ENDORSEMENT

Assessment Completed

I confirm that the candidate has demonstrated competence as an Advanced Instructor to the standards laid down by the RYA.

Venue

COASTAL/INLAND

Date

Approved by (RYA Coach/Assessor)

Signature

Name in capitals

KEELBOAT INSTRUCTOR ENDORSEMENT

Assessment Completed

I confirm that the candidate has demonstrated competence as a Keelboat Instructor to the standards laid down by the RYA.

Venue

COASTAL/INLAND

Date

Approved by (RYA Coach/Assessor)

Signature

Name in capitals

MULTIHULL INSTRUCTOR ENDORSEMENT

Assessment Completed

I confirm that the candidate has demonstrated competence as a Multihull Instructor to the standards laid down by the RYA.

Venue

COASTAL/INLAND

Date

Approved by (RYA Coach/Assessor)

Signature

Name in capitals

DINGHY INSTRUCTOR ENDORSEMENT

(For those whose initial instructor award is in keelboats or multihulls)

Assessment Completed

I confirm that the candidate has demonstrated competence as a Dinghy Instructor to the standards laid down by the RYA.

Venue

COASTAL/INLAND

Date

Approved by (RYA Coach/Assessor)

Signature

Name in capitals

RACING INSTRUCTOR ENDORSEMENT

Assessment Completed

I confirm that the candidate has demonstrated competence as a Racing Instructor to the standards laid down by the RYA.

Venue

COASTAL/INLAND

Date

Approved by (RYA Coach/Assessor)

Signature

Name in capitals

SENIOR INSTRUCTOR

Recommendation

I confirm that the candidate is competent to plan, organise and run a course within the RYA National Sailing Scheme.

Signature (Principal)

Signature

Name in capitals

Recognised Training Centre

Date

Eligibility

Minimum age 18

Two years intermittent or one year full time instructing since qualifying as a Dinghy Instructor is recommended.

RYA Safety Boat certificate or Level 4 certificate (pre-1996)

Valid first aid certificate of a type recognised by the Health and Safety Executive and covering the treatment of hypothermia.

Sailing ability to at least the standard of RYA Dinghy Instructor

Recommendation from Principal of an RYA training centre

Training Course

I confirm that the candidate has successfully completed the course and has demonstrated competence in all the areas required.

Venue

COASTAL/INLAND

Date

Signature (Course Organiser)

Signature

Name in capitals

RYA CLUB RACING COACH

Training course completed at (venue)

Date

Approved by (RYA/RRTC)

Signature

Name in capitals

Powerboat Level 2

Date of issue

First Aid Certificate

Signature

Type

Date of issue

Checked by (signature)

Signature

Name in capitals

Date

Revalidation

Revalidation is required every 3 years and you will need to present your Logbook, first aid certificate and power boat qualification.

Date	*Top Mark* Venue	Signature (High Performance Manager or Coaching Development Manager)

Class Racing Coach

1 Training Course

I can confirm that the candidate has attended the Class Racing Coaches Course

Venue   COASTAL/INLAND

Date

Signature (Class Racing Coach Tutor)   _Signature_

Name in capitals

2 Assessment by National Coach

I can confirm that the candidate has completed the assessment process and has proved to be an effective and skilled racing coach.

Venue   COASTAL/INLAND

Date

Signature (National Racing Coach)   _Signature_

Name in capitals

3 Attendance at National Top Mark

The candidate has attended an annual _Top Mark_

Venue   COASTAL/INLAND

Date

Signature (Coaching Developing Manager)   _Signature_

Name in capitals

4 The Award

The candidate has successfully completed all of the requirements laid down by the RYA and is awarded the Class Racing Coaching qualification.

Coaching Development Manager   _Signature_

Name in capitals

Revalidation

To be awarded every three years by attending the National *Top Mark*

Date	*Top Mark* Venue	Signature (High Performance Manager or Coaching Development Manager)

COACH/ASSESSOR

Recommendation

I confirm that the candidate has the experience and technical competence to be trained as a Coach/Assessor with the RYA National Sailing Scheme.

Regional Coach

Signature

Name in Capitals

Training Course

I confirm that the candidate has successfully completed the course and has demonstrated competence in all the areas required.

National Coach

Signature

Name in capitals

Details of dates, venue and conditions must be entered in the Personal Log on page 117

Task Experience

I confirm that the candidate has assisted with an RYA Instructor Course and Assessment.

RYA Coach/Assessor

Signature

Name in capitals

The candidate has completed all the requirements and is hereby appointed as an RYA Coach/Assessor.

RYA National Coach

Signature

Date

CHILD PROTECTION

Introduction

It is widely recognised that organisations working with children should take basic steps to ensure that the young people in their care are safe from harm. These steps are usually summarised in a Child Protection Policy, stating the club's or centre's intention to protect young people from harm, and Procedures outlining the simple steps to be followed. RYA Training Centres and clubs working with young people under 18 should have a Child Protection Policy and some simple Child Protection Procedures in place.

A blueprint policy and procedures, together with sample paperwork, is available on the RYA website www.rya.org.uk. These guidelines have been produced by the RYA to help your organisation take appropriate action to enable children and vulnerable adults to enjoy sailing, windsurfing and power boating in a safe environment. They are designed to help you to decide what paperwork and systems, if any, your organisation should adopt. They can be copied, quoted and adapted for club or centre use and are reviewed annually.

The RYA Policy Statement on Child Protection is as follows:

- The child's welfare is paramount.

- All children whatever their age, culture, disability, gender, language, racial origin, religious belief and/or sexual identity, have the right to protection from abuse.

- All suspicions and allegations of inappropriate behaviour will be taken seriously and responded to swiftly and appropriately.

- As defined in the Children Act 1989, anyone under the age of 18 years should be considered as a child for the purposes of this document.

Note for Principals - Good Recruitment Practice

If a good recruitment policy is adopted, and the issue of child protection covered in the organisation's risk assessment, both children and staff should be adequately protected. Abusers have great difficulty operating in a well-run organisation, with good quality management and training.

In general RYA Training centres should take up references on staff and volunteers, particularly where they may be working unsupervised. If there are concerns about a particular individual, a Criminal Records Bureau (CRB) check may be appropriate.

The aim of the CRB is to make justifiable levels of information available to people responsible for recruitment decisions so that they can decide for themselves if someone has an unsuitable background. An RYA Recognised or affiliated organisation can request a Disclosure Certificate on an individual through the RYA, which is a CRB registered umbrella body. The process is outlined more fully on the RYA website.

There have also been cases where allegations, which turned out to be unsubstantiated, have been made against an adult and have been difficult to disprove. If relevant Procedures are in place (such as discouraging instructors from working 1:1 and alone) it is very difficult for this kind of thing to happen.

Identifying Child Abuse

Child abuse, and particularly child sexual abuse, can arouse strong emotions in those facing such a situation and it is important to understand those feelings and not allow them to interfere with your professional judgement.

Alternatively a sailing instructor may identify a case where a child needs protection, particularly where children attend on a regular basis. Child abuse may come to light in a number of ways:

- A child may tell you what has happened to them
- From a third party (for example, another child)
- Through the child's behaviour
- A suspicious, unexplained injury to the child

The following brief notes provide a guide to help you identify signs of possible abuse and know what action to take in such cases. The RYA Child Protection Guidelines on the RYA website cover the subject more fully. If you are concerned about what is happening to a child, you may find the simple flow diagrams in these Guidelines helpful. They take you, step by step, through the actions which you should consider taking.

Forms of abuse

Physical abuse

This is where adults physically hurt or injure children and includes hitting, shaking, burning or biting etc. as well as giving children alcohol, inappropriate drugs or poison. Attempted suffocation or drowning also comes within this category.

Sexual abuse

Children are abused by adults who use children to meet their own sexual needs. This might be any form of sexual intercourse, masturbation, oral sex, or fondling. Showing children pornographic magazines or videos is also a form of sexual abuse.

Emotional abuse

Persistent lack of love and affection damages children emotionally. Being constantly shouted at, threatened or taunted can make the child very nervous and withdrawn.

Neglect

This is where an adult fails to meet a child's basic needs, like food or warm clothing. Children might also be constantly left alone unsupervised. Sometimes adults fail to, or refuse to, give their children love and affection. This is emotional neglect.

Abuse in all its forms can affect a child of any age. The effects can be so damaging that they may follow an individual into adulthood.

Identifying signs of possible abuse

Recognising abuse is not easy, even for individuals who have experience of working with child abuse. Most children will receive cuts, grazes and bruises from time to time and their behaviour may give reason for concern. There may well be other reasons for these factors other than abuse, but any concern should be immediately discussed with a senior colleague to assess the situation.

Warning signs which may alert instructors to the possibility of abuse can include

- Unexplained bruising, cuts or burns on the child, particularly if these are parts of the body not normally injured in accidents
- An injury which a parent or carer tries to hide, or for which they might have given different explanations

- Changes in behaviour such as the child suddenly becoming very quiet, tearful, withdrawn, aggressive, or displaying severe tantrums
- Loss of weight without a medical explanation
- An inappropriately dressed or ill-kept child who may also be dirty
- Sexually explicit behaviour, for instance playing games and showing awareness which is inappropriate for the child's age.
- Continual masturbation, aggressive and inappropriate sex play
- Running away from home, attempted suicides, self-inflicted injuries
- A lack of trust in adults, particularly those who would normally be close to the child
- Eating problems, including over-eating or loss of appetite

Remember, the above signs do not necessarily mean that a child has been abused. If you are concerned about the welfare of a child, however, you must act. Do not assume that someone else will help the child; they might not.

Listening to the child

Remember that the child's welfare is paramount, and this must be the most important consideration.

Listen carefully to any complaint or allegation by the child, and tell and show the child that you are taking them seriously.

If a child's behaviour or your observations give rise to concern, then talk to the child sensitively to find out if there is anything worrying them.

Keep questions to a minimum, but make sure you are absolutely clear about what a child has said so that you can pass on this information to professionals who are trained and experienced in investigating possible child abuse.

Acknowledge how difficult and painful it must have been for them to confide in you and reassure the child, stressing that they are never to blame.

Stay calm; don't take hasty or inappropriate action.

Don't make promises you may not be able to keep.

Don't take sole responsibility; consult a senior colleague so that together you can begin to protect the child, and also so that you can get some support for yourself in what could be a difficult situation.

As soon as possible after talking with the child, make a written record of what the child said, how they were behaving, and what you did in response.

Talking to parents and carers

It is possible that a relationship with parents and carers will have been established and as a general principle it is important to be open and honest when dealing with them.

There may be circumstances, however, when it is not appropriate for parents to be informed immediately of the concerns you have, as this may prejudice any investigation and may place the child at even greater risk.

Always discuss your concerns first with a senior colleague; contact with parents could be delayed until you have sought advice from one of the professional agencies who have been notified (see below).

Responding to child abuse; what to do if you are concerned

Remember that it is not your responsibility to decide if child abuse has occurred, but it is your responsibility to take action, however small your concern.

Inform a senior colleague, (there may be a designated person for the role), who will take responsibility for seeking any additional advice and for contacting the local Social Services Department, the Police or the NSPCC. These organisations are trained to deal with such situations and have the necessary legal power to protect the child.

If no senior colleagues are available, or concerns for the child remain, then you must contact the local Social Services Department, the Police or the NSPCC yourself. You do not have to give your name, although this will be helpful to the agency making enquiries into the matter and who may need to talk to you again.

The agency receiving your referral will take responsibility for ensuring that appropriate investigations are undertaken and the child protected.

Allegations of abuse against members of staff

Child abuse can and does occur outside the family setting, although it is a sensitive and difficult issue, child abuse has occurred within institutions and may occur in other settings.

It is important for Principals to review the operation of their centres to minimise the situations where any adult is left alone with a child (or group of very young children).

What to do if there are allegations of abuse against a member of staff

Again, remember it is the child's welfare which must be of paramount importance.

Follow the guidelines in the section dealing with 'Listening to the Child' and consult the RYA Child Protection guidelines.

Refer the matter to a senior colleague so that the appropriate child protection procedures can be followed. The senior member of staff must inform the Social Services Department, the Police or the NSPCC.

If your concern is about a senior colleague, then seek advice from another senior member of staff who should ensure that the child protection procedures are implemented and the Social Services Department, the Police or the NSPCC are informed.

It is important to understand that a member of staff reporting a case of child abuse, particularly by a colleague, may undergo a very high degree of stress, including feelings of guilt for having reported the matter. It is therefore very important to ensure that appropriate counselling and support is available for staff in such a situation.

APPEALS PROCEDURE

Assessment standards

All RYA-qualified Instructors and Assessors are required to treat students and candidates with respect and fairness.

All assessments in the use of boats and their equipment have implications for the safety of participants. It is therefore essential that candidates be given a thorough and searching assessment. It would be dangerous to the candidate and anyone whom they subsequently teach if an Assessor erred on the side of leniency in awarding a certificate. There must never be any question of relaxing the standards required for an award.

Realistic aims

In some cases, it becomes clear to the Assessor at an early stage in the assessment process that the candidate has been over-ambitious in their choice of award. In such instances the Assessor should discuss the situation with the candidate and agree revised achievable aims.

Grounds for appeal

A candidate has grounds for appeal if he or she believes:

Either   That they have not been given a reasonable opportunity to demonstrate their competence.

Or

That the person carrying out the assessment has placed them under undue or unfair pressure.

Or

That the Assessor has reached the wrong conclusion on the basis of the outcome of the candidate's performance in the assessment.

The procedure

The candidate should first raise the concern with the Assessor to see if the matter can be amicably resolved. If it is inappropriate to consult the Assessor, or if there is no amicable solution, the candidate should appeal in writing to the RYA National Coach within 20 working days of the assessment. The letter of appeal should contain the following:

- Full details of the assessment - when, where, involving whom etc
- The nature of the appeal
- Any supporting documentation relating to the assessment - outcome, action plans, reports etc.

On receipt of an appeal, an investigative process will commence. Following investigation, the candidate will be informed of the outcome, which will be one of the following:

- The original decision confirmed
- The assessment carried out again by the same or a different Assessor
- The original decision overturned and the assessment judged to be adequate

If the candidate is still unhappy about the decision, they may appeal against the outcome to the RYA Training Divisional Committee.

GLOSSARY

ABACK	The sail pressed backwards by the wind
ABAFT	Behind the boat
ABEAM	At right angles to the line of the boat
ADRIFT	Afloat, but without a propulsive force
AFT	Towards back of the boat
AGROUND	On the ground and not afloat
AHEAD	The area in front of the boat
AMIDSHIPS	In the middle of the boat
AWASH	The boat being full of water
BACKING	The wind changing direction in an anti-clockwise direction (against the sun)
BALANCE	How level the boat is
BEAM	The side of a boat
BEARING AWAY	Changing direction away from the wind
BELAY	Twist a rope around something to make fast
BELLY OF THE SAIL	The fullness of the sail
BIGHT	A loop
BLANKETING	To take the wind from another craft which is to leeward
BOTTLE SCREW	A means of attaching and adjusting shrouds
BROACHING	To turn sideways onto the wind and heel over
BURGEE	A flag
BY THE LEE	Sailing with the wind on the same side of the boat as the mainsail
CABLE	A nautical measurement being 200 yards or 100 fathoms
CASTING OFF	Leaving the moorings
CARS	Adjustable fairleads on tracks, to adjust sheet angle
CATSPAWS	Ripples on the surface of the water showing a gust of wind
CHAIN PLATE	Metal plate to which the shrouds are attached at their base
CLAWING OFF	Sailing off a Lee shore
COAMING	The built up woodwork around hatches etc to exclude water
CRINGLE	The metal ring used to reinforce any holes in the sail
CROSS TREES	Horizontal spreaders which hold the shrouds away from the mast
CUNNINGHAM	System for tensioning luff of sail
DISPLACEMENT	The amount of water that a boat displaces (Archimedes' Principle)

DOWNHAUL	See Cunningham
TO EASE	To slacken
EBB	At tide is on the ebb when it is falling
EDDY	A current flowing in a different direction to the main stream
FAIRLEADS	Permanent fixtures on a boat which are designed to guide a rope
FAIRWAY	A clear passage for navigation
FALL	The loose end of a rope
FATHOM	A measurement of depth (1 fathom = 6 feet)
FLOOD	A flooding tide is a rising one
FREEBOARD	The amount of boat above the water line
GHOSTING	To move when there is no recognisable wind
GNAV	Lever above boom, function same as kicker
HEADWAY	Forward momentum
HEAT SEALING	Tidy end of rope by melting together
HOUNDS	The fixture of the mast to which the shrouds are attached
IN IRONS, STAYS	The boat lies head to wind, sails flapping
JURY RIG	This is an emergency rig, having undergone temporary repair
KICKER	(Kicking strap) pulley system between boom and mast designed to tension leech of sail
LUFF	To change the boat's direction towards the wind
MAKE FAST	To secure
MAST STEP	The slot into which the mast heel fits
OUTHAUL	System for tensioning foot of sail
RACKS	Metal or carbon extensions to side of boat
ROCKER	Amount of curve on the longitudinal axis at bottom of the boat
RAKE	Angle of mast to vertical
SPLICE	To tidy end of rope by weaving through itself
TELL TALE	Wool or lightweight tape used to detect airflow
TRIM	Fore and aft adjustment of weight in boat
VANG	See KICKER
VEERING	The wind changing direction in a clockwise direction (with the sun)
WARP	Rope used for anchoring or mooring
WEIGHING	Raising the anchor
WHIPPING	End of rope tidied by winding twine around it